T0077878

THE MESSIAH'S IMMINENT RETURN

ARE YOU READY?

DELINDA N. BAKER

Scripture Teaching and Bible Study

WESTBOW
PRESS®
A DIVISION OF THOMAS NELSON
& ZONDERVAN

WestBow Press books may be ordered through booksellers or by contacting:

WestBow Press
A Division of Thomas Nelson & Zondervan
1663 Liberty Drive
Bloomington, IN 47403
www.westbowpress.com
1 (866) 928-1240

ISBN: 978-1-9736-0593-5 (sc)
ISBN: 978-1-9736-0595-9 (hc)
ISBN: 978-1-9736-0594-2 (e)

Library of Congress Control Number: 2017916605

Print information available on the last page.

WestBow Press rev. date: 11/13/2017

ACKNOWLEDGMENTS

I am deeply appreciative of the support and feedback I have received while putting this book together. My pastor, Roger DeYoung, has stood by my side during the development and outline of the materials and provided support and counsel. My dear friends, Amy and Lois, provided input on the overall structure and biblical accuracy of the text. Proverbs 15:22 says, "Plans fail for lack of counsel, but with many advisers they succeed." I am very fortunate to have such a strong Bible-believing family, friends, and church supporting me.

To those in my family who for generations have gone before me planting the seed of knowledge of Jesus Christ, faith and obedience to the one true God, and the hope of salvation and eternal life through the power of his resurrection.

CONTENTS

INTRODUCTION

What will it be like when Jesus returns to earth? I've spent a great deal of time contemplating this wondrous event and what it will be like. If what the Bible teaches is true, can you imagine the unspeakable joy of those who have followed Jesus and his teachings when they see him returning in the sky? In one second, their faith will be validated and their suffering will end. They will be on the winning side! Their Lord and Savior will be victorious, and all the enemies of God will be defeated.

At the same time, can you imagine the terror and angst of those who have denied him? They will realize in one second they have chosen the wrong path and the wrong leader. They will be on the losing side. Much of what they've stood for will be undone. God's ways will prevail and humanity's ungodly ways will end.

The Bible says this event will be witnessed by the entire world. With today's technology, that is entirely possible and probable. Since Christians believe this will happen, we must ask ourselves, what is the correct response to this prophetic insight?

Typical of humanity's inquisitive nature, the first thing people generally want to know is when this will happen. In this way, we are no different from the disciples over 2,000 years ago. When Jesus told his disciples he would someday rule this earth, they asked him when it would occur and what they should expect. Jesus told them what to look for in the days leading up to his return and how to endure and overcome the difficulties of those final days.

Other prophecies in the Old and New Testament also add insight to the when, where, and who of this momentous event, but that is not all we find in scriptures. As important as these details are, one other important insight that is given is how we should prepare for and live in the days leading up to the Messiah's return. It is not God's intent that we just wait for his return; rather, we have an important role to play in the end days.

The objective of this book is to look at Jesus's response to his disciples and the prophecies and signs pointing to the Messiah's return, to clarify the end-time events we should watch for and to prepare Christians for the coming days.

This book looks at these events from a Christian perspective; it presumes Jesus Christ is the Messiah prophesied in the Old Testament who has already come to this earth as Savior and who will return as Lord and ruler. Also for the purposes of this book, the Messiah's second coming refers to the Messiah's return to rule the earth, not to the rapture of the saints.

Many scholars have attempted to interpret the signs and understand current and historical events as they relate to the days preceding the Messiah's return. These have included notable authors such as Billy Graham, David Jeremiah, Tim LaHaye, and many others. There are almost as many different outlooks and interpretations of these events as there are authors. So how do we know which interpretation is correct? Is there one author or outlook that is more correct than the others?

To try to answer this, let us reflect for a minute on Jesus's first coming as a humble child and Savior. Many priests and scholars at the time of Jesus's birth had studied the Old Testament scriptures and prophecies. Like scholars today, they strove to interpret the scriptures and anticipate the Messiah's coming. Yet few recognized Jesus as the Messiah when he came to earth as a man and Savior.

Even those close to Jesus had difficulty fully understanding his divine nature. At Jesus's baptism, John the Baptist spiritually discerned Jesus was the Messiah. He said, "I need to be baptized by you, and do you come to me?" (Matthew 3:14). John was also given additional firsthand evidence after Jesus's baptism as he witnessed "the Spirit of God descending like a dove and alighting on him" and heard "a voice from heaven" saying "This is my Son, whom I love; with him I am well pleased" (Matthew 3:16–17). Yet with all this insight and eyewitness of events, this same John later began to question whether Jesus was the Messiah as he sat in a jail cell. In Matthew 11:3, John asked, "Are you the one who is to come, or should we expect someone else?"

John was not alone in his questioning. Jesus's disciples and the early church had difficulty fully understanding the prophecies as well. Jesus often explained the scriptures to enlighten his followers. Later, Paul admitted his human limitations in a letter to the church in Corinth: "For now we see only a reflection as in a mirror; then we shall see face to face. Now I know in part; then I shall know fully, even as I am fully known" (1 Corinthians 13:12).

Why were they confused when Jesus was in their presence? Possibly because prophecies often provide a general outline of events to come with timetables that can span months or centuries, but they do not always provide specific details.

It is much easier to interpret prophecy fulfilled than prophecy yet to come; hindsight is 20/20. But prophecy has an important role in our faith; it validates God's overarching plan and sets forth a promise that our trust and hope in him is not in vain. So even if it is difficult, we must do our best to understand and respond to the prophecies we've been given.

With that in mind and with a great deal of humility, in this book, we will . . .

- search the scriptures to see what the prophets and Jesus have foreshadowed,
- look at historical events that most scholars agree are significant concerning the fulfillment of these prophecies, and
- seek to understand how we should live while we wait for the blessed return of Jesus as Lord and King.

We will not . . .

- be dogmatic about how to interpret the signs or the timing of the events, nor will we promote one viewpoint over another, and

- cover the seal, bowl, and horn judgments in the book of Revelation. Only the sections of Revelation pertaining to Jesus's return will be addressed.

Together, we will walk through the scriptures and events. Scripture text is provided to enable readers to see the referenced scriptures in context. There is no greater truth or teacher than the Word of God.

As we go over the scriptures related to the return of the Messiah, we have a lot of material to look at. According to David Jeremiah,

> References to the Second Coming outnumber references to the first by a factor of eight to one. Scholars have identified 1,845 biblical references to the Second Coming. In the Old Testament, Christ's return is emphasized in no less than seventeen books, and New Testament authors speak of it in twenty-three of the twenty-seven books.[1]

The fact that Christ's second coming features so prominently in scripture is an indication that this event is important to God—and consequently, it should also be important to us.

Since some prophecies have already come to perfect fruition, this gives us further assurance as to the accuracy and validity of the remaining unfulfilled events. The question regarding these prophecies isn't whether but when these events will occur. Also, as we look to the future, our emphasis should be on both the prophesied events and on the body of Christ and its state of preparation and readiness for those events. Both are important.

Outline for Book

We will begin our study of the Messiah's imminent return by a review of God's promises expressed through covenants with Israel and humanity throughout the Old Testament. This is foundational to our understanding of the end times. Through the covenants, we discover that nothing that has occurred or is yet to occur is accidental. Our God is all powerful and in control of heavenly and earthly events. Furthermore, he is a God of purpose.

Next, we will review Old Testament prophecies written hundreds of years prior to Jesus's first coming including Ezekiel, Isaiah, Daniel, and several minor prophets. These will give us insight into the who, what, when, and where of events leading up to and including Jesus's return as King.

Finally, we will look at what Jesus, his apostles, and the early church taught about future events. By being as close to the Lord's first coming and Jesus's direct teachings as recorded, we hope to add insight to our understanding of these events. After all, how much closer can we get to the author of these events than through God-incarnate in Jesus Christ?

My goal is to provide a comprehensive foundation and understanding of scriptures related to the Messiah's return to rule the earth. This will educate Christians as they sift through all the contemporary movies, sermons, and phenomena surrounding this topic to help them distinguish truth from fiction and guide them as they set their priorities on the things that matter.

PART 1

OLD TESTAMENT TEACHINGS ON END TIMES

CHAPTER 1

A GOD OF COVENANTS

I make known the end from the beginning, from
ancient times, what is still to come. I say, "My purpose
will stand, and I will do all that I please."
—Isaiah 46:10

Every day, the news seems to be punctuated by some new catastrophe—financial unrest, natural disasters, wars, terrorist attacks, on and on. Today's norm is instability, anger, and fear as we watch our dreams of a peaceful, prosperous existence evaporate.

In 2015, we watched the stock market drop over a thousand points and heard that China's market was on the brink of faltering. Countries such as Greece have gone broke needing international loans to rescue them while other countries struggle with increasing national debt.

There have been major tsunamis, earthquakes, volcanic eruptions, and other natural disasters around the globe that have killed thousands. The world seems to be reeling from one natural disaster after another while others are predicted and seemed poised to occur in the near future.

Terrorist attacks are rampant. We see bombs exploding and shootings of innocent victims in gathering spots throughout Europe. Israel is under constant threat from its neighbors, and occasionally, like moles, Palestinians break through the protective walls surrounding the nation by digging tunnels. But lest we think all of this unrest is only abroad and that somehow we are safe in the United States, we should keep in mind the 9/11 attacks.

Even the church is not immune. We hear of persecution of the church in various parts of the world. In 2015, the cruel beheading of twenty-one Coptic Christians was posted on YouTube for the world to view.[2] In addition, other Christians have been beheaded and persecuted in the Middle East for their beliefs. Not long ago, *Christianity Today* reported that over 400 crosses had been removed from buildings of worship in China.[3] In the United States, we see increasing animosity toward Christians, a twisting and distortion of God's Word, and Supreme Court rulings that challenge our basic beliefs.

With the growing intensity of signs that have long been recognized as predecessors of the Messiah's return, it is only natural to ask if the time for the Messiah's return is growing near.

Billy Graham referred to all these events as "storm warnings." In his book by the same title, he wrote,

> Storm warnings of a different sort cannot be ignored—storm warnings from the Bible urging us to pay attention to the crises in our world, leading us to the final events that must take place before Jesus Christ comes again. These storms, the Bible says, will be of apocalyptic proportions—disasters that will shatter even the foundations of human society.[4]

Even national leaders seem to have prophetic insights to an approaching storm. President Bush, in his 1992 State of the Union Address, spoke of the undeniable awareness that something profound and unusual was happening to the world; "big changes," he called them. Midway through his address, the President warned of the dangers still ahead with striking words:

The world is still a dangerous place. Only the dead have seen the end of conflict. And though yesterday's challenges are behind us, tomorrow's are being born.[5]

Understanding Covenants

When we talk about end-time events, those events preceding the Messiah's return, it is important that we begin by putting these events in the perspective of God's overarching plan. The Messiah's return and all related current and future events that precede it are not random events. Instead, these events have been prophesied and anticipated for centuries. They are leading up to the fulfillment of God's promises as outlined in covenants he has given to his people.

> The Messiah's return and all related current and future events that precede it are not random events.

Beth Moore refers to this as providence—a plan and purpose for his world.

> Providence is not a principle or orderliness or reason; rather, providence is the will of the Creator who is actively involved in moving his creation to a goal. History is not a cyclical process of endless repetition; history is being moved toward the predetermined end.[6]

Another term related to this concept is eschatology, what the Bible teaches about the future. Often as we read the Old Testament, we see visions of what the future will hold for us. To validate the accuracy of such predictions, these long-term prophetic visions will usually be given side by side with short-term visions that will be fulfilled in the lifetime of those who give them. The uncompromising test of a prophet in the

Bible is total accuracy. "If what a prophet proclaims in the name of the Lord does not take place or come true, that is a message the Lord has not spoken" (Deuteronomy 18:22).

And how are eschatological (future) providential (predetermined) plans made known to us? This can be done in a number of ways—through visions and dreams, through angelic messengers, and through covenants. *Webster's* defines a covenant as "a written agreement or promise usually under seal between two or more parties especially for the performance of some action."[7] In the Old Testament, the Hebrew word for covenant is *berit.* This word is used in scripture for a variety of oath-bound commitments in various relationships.

Furthermore, covenants between God and his people are more than just contracts; they are relational in nature. Covenants between God and humanity are based on a presumption of faithfulness and loyalty. A great example of this faith-love relationship between humanity and God is in Psalm 117:1–2: "Praise the Lord, all you nations; extol him, all you peoples. For great is his love toward us, and the faithfulness of the Lord endures forever." The Hebrew words used here for love and faithfulness are *hesed* and *emet.* Hesed has to do with showing kindness in loyal love, and emet can be translated as faithfulness or truth.

> Covenants between God and his people are more than just contracts; they are relational in nature.

This is amazing. The God who created the universe, who knows every component of how his creation works from massive solar systems to the cells in the creatures he's made to live in them, this same God who is beyond our understanding desires to have a relationship with us all.

Covenants also form a bond between God and humanity—a promise. God sees the future and knows when the end will be. He has planned the path, guaranteed its fulfillment, and lovingly shown us the way.

Types of Covenants

Before we start looking at the key covenants in the Old Testament, let's look at the types of contracts or agreements commonly used in scripture.

The first type of contract was called a royal grant treaty and was akin to an unconditional gift. It was a promissory agreement—one that conveyed or implied a promise that arose out of a king's desire to reward a servant. Examples of biblical covenants of this type include those made with Abraham and David in which God established unconditional covenants with them impacting generations to come.

The second type of contract was more-relational in nature. In terms not commonly used today, it was called a suzerain-vassal treaty; it bound an inferior vassal to a superior suzerain. Vassals were those under the protection of a feudal lord to whom they had vowed respect, honor, and intense fidelity; they were in a subordinate position.

On the other hand, a suzerain could have been an overlord or a dominant region controlling the foreign relations of a vassal state while allowing it sovereign authority in its internal affairs. Hence, suzerain-vassal covenants recognized God's superiority over humanity and its subservient position. Examples of these types of covenants include those made with Adam, Noah, and Moses in which God clearly established his sovereignty over them.

Some folks also attempt to categorize covenants as conditional or unconditional though this is not always easy to do. If they are unconditional, regardless of our obedience or disobedience, God will fulfill them. If they are conditional, the covenant will bring either blessings or curses depending on our response of obedience or disobedience.

Finally, while some covenants in the Old Testament were made only with Israel, others were made with humanity in general.

Covenants of the Old Testament

There are six to eight recognized covenants in the Old Testament. There is the covenant made at creation with God and humanity. There are the covenants made with Adam, Noah, Abraham, and with God's people after their deliverance from Egypt (referred to as the Palestinian Land covenant) that outline the promise for God's people. There is the covenant made with Moses at Mount Sinai outlining righteous living. And there are the covenants given to David and Jeremiah relating to the future prosperity of Israel. Let's become familiar with each of these.

Edenic (Creation) Covenant

The first covenant God made with humanity was in the garden of Eden in Genesis 1:28–29. While not everyone recognizes this covenant as separate from the covenant made a few chapters later with Adam, all agree this is the first scripture to establish God's original plan of human responsibility toward creation.

> [28] God blessed them and said to them, "Be fruitful and increase in number; fill the earth and subdue it. Rule over the fish in the sea and the birds in the sky and over every living creature that moves on the ground." [29] Then God said, "I give you every seed-bearing plant on the face of the whole earth and every tree that has fruit with seed in it. They will be yours for food." (Genesis 1:28–29)

God intended for humanity to rule over the animals and subdue them and take care of God's garden. God would provide food for them and the animals from the plants of the earth. But there was one constraint found in Genesis 2:17—humanity was not to "eat from the tree of the knowledge of good and evil, for when you eat from it you will certainly die."

Of course, Adam and Eve did exactly what they had been told not to do; they ate from the forbidden tree, were punished, and were kicked out of the garden. I suppose the relationship between humanity and God could have ended there and this would have been a tale of defeat and hopelessness. But don't forget the hesed-emet nature of God, that is, the loyal love and faithful relationship at the core of his covenants. God in His grace continued to show love and forbearance to humanity. After the fall, this covenant was augmented by subsequent covenants with Adam, Noah, and Abraham.

In summary, the creation covenant

- was made with humanity,
- was conditional—humanity could not eat from the tree of the knowledge of good and evil without consequence,
- established God's rule and relationship to humanity, and
- outlined humanity's responsibility for creation.

Adamic Covenant

The consequence that humanity was warned about in the creation covenant had been realized. It is typical of humanity to try to remove or avoid the consequences of its actions. But this is not usually how we see God work. Consequence is inevitable when we sin and is a powerful teacher that shapes us.

In Genesis 3:14–19, we find an amendment to the creation covenant. This covenant contains the cursed state of man, which creation must now endure because of Adam's fall.

> [14] So the LORD God said to the serpent, "Because you have done this, Cursed are you above all livestock and all wild animals! You will crawl on your belly and you will eat dust all the days of your life. [15] And I will put enmity between you and the woman, and between your offspring and hers; he will crush your head, and you will

strike his heel." ¹⁶ To the woman he said, "I will make your pains in childbearing very severe; with painful labor you will give birth to children. Your desire will be for your husband, and he will rule over you."

¹⁷ To Adam he said, "Because you listened to your wife and ate fruit from the tree about which I commanded you, 'You must not eat from it,' Cursed is the ground because of you; through painful toil you will eat food from it all the days of your life. ¹⁸ It will produce thorns and thistles for you, and you will eat the plants of the field. ¹⁹ By the sweat of your brow you will eat your food until you return to the ground, since from it you were taken; for dust you are and to dust you will return." (Genesis 3:14–19)

The Adamic covenant might be considered a suzerain-vassal treaty since it was issued by God, who judges humanity. There is nothing we can do to change the outcome of this curse, so it would be considered unconditional. Difficult labor to cultivate and reap from the earth's produce, pain in childbirth, and man's dominance over woman would be a way of life on this earth.

While humanity has tried to break free from this curse by its own effort through technological advances and women's liberation, this is clearly an ongoing battle worldwide. But the most devastating result of the curse that none of us can escape is death. In Eden, death was not a part of God's plan. But now, to contain our sin and its outcome, death has entered the world.

In the midst of the curse or punishment given to disobedient man, God mercifully provides hope. In verse 15, we see our first glimpse at the future Savior: "And I will put enmity between you and the woman, and between your offspring and hers; he will crush your head, and you will strike his heel." From the day humanity sinned, God providentially made a plan to deliver it back into the original relationship he desired and lovingly intended for it.

The offspring prophetically referenced here is the Messiah, who will someday come and defeat Satan. With the Messiah's first coming, we saw him defeat the finality of death with his resurrection. We will see this plan culminated when the Lord comes in power and glory to rule the earth and defeat Satan once and for all.

In summary, this covenant

- was made with humanity,
- was unconditional,
- was initiated due to Adam's sin,
- outlined the cursed state of humanity and creation, and
- anticipated God's future provision for that sin.

Noahic Covenant

Several generations followed the covenant made with Adam. Humanity had fallen into deep sin with the exception of one man. Judgment was inevitable. After destroying humanity with a worldwide flood, in Genesis 8:20–22, God renewed his covenant with Noah and his family, the only survivors, and the remnant seed for future generations of humanity. The Noahic covenant restated God's authority over humanity and its duties as found in the Adamic covenant.

> [20] Then Noah built an altar to the LORD and, taking some of all the clean animals and clean birds, he sacrificed burnt offerings on it. [21] The LORD smelled the pleasing aroma and said in his heart: "Never again will I curse the ground because of humans, even though every inclination of the human heart is evil from childhood. And never again will I destroy all living creatures, as I have done. [22] As long as the earth endures, seedtime and harvest, cold and heat, summer and winter, day and night will never cease." (Genesis 8:20–22)

In Genesis 9:2–3, the covenant further expanded humanity's dominance over animals. Animals would dread and fear humanity, which could eat animals. In verses 6–7, God reconfirmed the value of human life, punishment for murderers, and the command to be fruitful and multiply.

> [2] The fear and dread of you will fall on all the beasts of the earth, and on all the birds in the sky, on every creature that moves along the ground, and on all the fish in the sea; they are given into your hands. [3] Everything that lives and moves about will be food for you. Just as I gave you the green plants, I now give you everything … [6] Whoever sheds human blood, by humans shall their blood be shed; for in the image of God has God made mankind. [7] As for you, be fruitful and increase in number; multiply on the earth and increase upon it. (Genesis 9:2–3, 6–7)

Finally, in Genesis 9:11, this covenant included a promise to never again destroy the world through a flood—"I establish my covenant with you: Never again will all life be destroyed by the waters of a flood; never again will there be a flood to destroy the earth." This is sometimes referred to as the rainbow promise since a rainbow will be set in the sky as a sign. In verse 16, the Lord said, "Whenever the rainbow appears in the clouds, I will see it and remember the everlasting covenant between God and all living creatures of every kind on the earth."

This covenant would be considered a suzerain-vassal treaty in that God established the terms of the treaty with humanity. There is nothing humanity or animals can do to alter the terms of this treaty; it is not conditional on humanity's response or lack of response.

In summary, this covenant

- was made with humanity,
- was unconditional,
- restated God's authority over humanity and its duties,

- added animosity between humanity and animals including eating flesh,
- established punishment for murderers, and
- stated God's promise to never again destroy the world through a flood (the rainbow promise).

Abrahamic Covenant

For the first time in Genesis 15:4–21, we see God narrowing his covenant from all humanity to a select people—Abraham and his descendants, then to Isaac, his son, his descendants, and ultimately Isaac's son, Jacob, who was renamed Israel. It is a royal grant covenant that was given to Abraham in recognition of his loyal and faithful obedience to God. Three key provisions of the covenant are land, the seed of a nation, and a blessing.

> [4] Then the word of the LORD came to him: "This man will not be your heir, but a son who is your own flesh and blood will be your heir." [5] He took him outside and said, "Look up at the sky and count the stars—if indeed you can count them." Then he said to him, "So shall your offspring be." ... [18] On that day the LORD made a covenant with Abram and said, "To your descendants I give this land, from the Wadi of Egypt to the great river, the Euphrates— [19] the land of the Kenites, Kenizzites, Kadmonites, [20] Hittites, Perizzites, Rephaites, [21] Amorites, Canaanites, Girgashites and Jebusites." (Genesis 15:4–5, 18–20)

In Genesis 17:10–11, the practice of circumcision was established, which was humanity's acknowledgment of the agreement and special relationship God had with his people. God told Abraham, "Every male among you shall be circumcised. You are to undergo circumcision, and it will be the sign of the covenant between me and you."

Every blessing experienced by the redeemed in Israel and the Christian church flows from this covenant. In Genesis 12:3, God promised that the families of the world would be blessed through Abraham: "I will bless those who bless you, and whoever curses you I will curse; and all peoples on earth will be blessed through you."

God promised Abraham that he would make his name great, that Abraham would have numerous physical descendants, and that he would be the father of a multitude of nations. He also laid out the geographical boundaries of the land his descendants would inherit. And he promised to bless the peoples of the earth through Abraham.

In summary, this covenant

- was made with Abraham and his descendants,
- was unconditional,
- stated that Abraham would be the father of a multitude of nations,
- outlined geographical boundaries of the nation of Israel, and
- promised a blessing to the world through his seed.

Mount Sinai (Mosaic) Covenant

The covenant on Mount Sinai was made exclusively with the descendants of Israel and is in Deuteronomy 11:26–28. It was a conditional covenant designed to teach God's people, who had been set apart, on how they might please God as his chosen nation. It brought God's blessing for obedience or his curse for disobedience.

> [26] See, I am setting before you today a blessing and a curse—[27] the blessing if you obey the commands of the LORD your God that I am giving you today; [28] the curse if you disobey the commands of the LORD your God and turn from the way that I command you today by following other gods, which you have not known. (Deuteronomy 11:26–28)

Exodus 20:1–17 outlines the Ten Commandments given to Moses on Mount Sinai, but this covenant also includes all the other laws outlined in Exodus and Deuteronomy. Over 600 commands are included in this covenant. In Exodus 24:8, Moses reaffirmed that this covenant was with God's chosen people when he stated, "This is the blood of the covenant that the LORD has made with you in accordance with all these words."

Later through the new covenant, Jesus replaced the conditions of the law with forgiveness through grace. At Jesus's last supper with his disciples before his crucifixion, he said, "This is my blood of the covenant, which is poured out for many for the forgiveness of sins" (Matthew 26:28). The curse of the law does not apply to Christians, who are forgiven and whose sins are covered by the sacrifice Jesus made on the cross.

In summary, this covenant

- was made with the nation of Israel,
- was conditional,
- included the Ten Commandments (Exodus 20:1–17) and over 600 commands (the Law), and
- outlined a blessing for obedience and a curse for disobedience.

Palestinian (Land) Covenant

In Deuteronomy 30:1–5, God made an additional covenant referred to as the land covenant with the Israelites after their miraculous departure from Egypt. As Moses revealed God's covenant at the foot of Mount Sinai, the land promise made centuries earlier with Abraham (Genesis 15) was confirmed. The boundaries of this land and rights of ownership have been the root of many wars and conflicts with Israel and the Palestinians as the people of Israel have sought to obtain and keep this land.

> ² And when you and your children return to the LORD
> your God and obey him with all your heart and with

all your soul according to everything I command you today, [3] then the LORD your God will restore your fortunes and have compassion on you and gather you again from all the nations where he scattered you … [5] He will bring you to the land that belonged to your ancestors, and you will take possession of it. He will make you more prosperous and numerous than your ancestors. (Deuteronomy 30:2–3, 5)

In verse 3, God reminded the Israelites that if they were disobedient and chased after other gods, they would be dispersed as a people. Though we saw some major defeats of Israel by the Assyrians in the eighth century BC and by the Babylonians in the sixth century BC, the full dispersion of the people of Israel occurred in AD 70.

This covenant also foreshadowed God's restoration of Israel as a nation (v. 5), which did not occur for almost 1,900 years. Israel was reestablished as a nation in 1948.

And finally, the covenant foresaw Israel's ultimate obedience, at which time God would cause them to prosper. In verses 9–10, Moses delivered God's promise,

[9] . . . The LORD will again delight in you [Israel] and make you prosperous, just as he delighted in your ancestors, [10] if you obey the LORD your God and keep his commands and decrees that are written in this Book of the Law and turn to the LORD your God with all your heart and with all your soul. (Deuteronomy 30:9-10)

It is the promise of ultimate prosperity and success that gives Israel hope as the time of the Messiah's return comes closer.

In summary, this covenant

- was made with the nation of Israel,
- was conditional (dispersion) and unconditional (promise of restoration),

- expanded on the Abrahamic covenant, and
- prophesied the future of Israel—dispersion due to disobedience and eventual restoration and prosperity.

Davidic Covenant

The covenant with David is the foundation for the future millennial kingdom. Through the prophet Nathan, God promised an eternal kingdom to David, his faithful servant whom he loved.

> [8] Now then, tell my servant David, "This is what the Lord Almighty says: I took you from the pasture, from tending the flock, and appointed you ruler over my people Israel. [9] I have been with you wherever you have gone, and I have cut off all your enemies from before you. Now I will make your name great, like the names of the greatest men on earth. [10] And I will provide a place for my people Israel and will plant them so that they can have a home of their own and no longer be disturbed. Wicked people will not oppress them anymore, as they did at the beginning [11] and have done ever since the time I appointed leaders over my people Israel. I will also give you rest from all your enemies. The Lord declares to you that the Lord himself will establish a house for you: [12] When your days are over and you rest with your ancestors, I will raise up your offspring to succeed you, your own flesh and blood, and I will establish his kingdom. [13] He is the one who will build a house for my Name, and I will establish the throne of his kingdom forever … [16] Your house and your kingdom will endure forever before me; your throne will be established forever." (2 Samuel 7: 8–13, 16)

It is a royal grant treaty that promises three things—posterity to the Davidic line, that his throne would be symbolic of royal authority, and an eternal kingdom on earth. God promised David that one of his descendants (Jesus) would rule on a throne as king forever.

In summary, this covenant

- was made with the nation of Israel,
- was unconditional,
- promised David's lineage would be forever,
- was the foundation for millennial promises, and
- prophesied that David's descendant would be on the throne and rule as king.

New Covenant

The last of the covenants in the Old Testament is the new covenant. This covenant was given to Jeremiah, referred to the future regeneration of Israel, and provided for the forgiveness of sins. It was first made with Israel and ultimately expanded to include the church. In the new covenant, God promised to forgive sin and foresaw a time when there would be a universal knowledge of the Lord in a future kingdom. While Jeremiah 31:31–34 is the most common reference, other conditions and provisions of the new covenant can also be found in Ezekiel and Isaiah as well.

> [31] "The days are coming," declares the LORD, "when I will make a new covenant with the people of Israel and with the people of Judah. [32] It will not be like the covenant I made with their ancestors when I took them by the hand to lead them out of Egypt, because they broke my covenant, though I was a husband to them," declares the LORD. [33] "This is the covenant I will make with the people of Israel after that time," declares the LORD. "I will put my law in their minds and write it on their hearts. I will be their God, and they will be my people. [34] No longer will they teach their neighbor, or

say to one another, 'Know the LORD,' because they will all know me, from the least of them to the greatest," declares the LORD. "For I will forgive their wickedness and will remember their sins no more." (Jeremiah 31:31–34)

Since Jesus has already come to earth as a Savior and redeemed his people, Gentiles and Jews who choose to follow Him are under the new covenant and are free from the penalty of the Law. As Paul stated in Ephesians 2:8–9, "For it is by grace you have been saved, through faith—and this is not from yourselves, it is the gift of God—not by works, so that no one can boast."

In summary, this covenant

- was made initially with the nation of Israel and later extended to the followers of Jesus (Christians),
- was unconditional,
- reaffirmed the future regeneration of Israel,
- provided for the forgiveness of sins, and
- prophesied a future universal knowledge of the Lord.

Dispensation versus Covenant Theology

In review of the covenants made by God to his people, there are two approaches to understanding their meaning and intended recipients— covenant theology and dispensation theology.

Covenant theology teaches there is a common covenant of grace for believers, there is one church that includes all Christians (both converted Jews and Gentiles), and there will ultimately be unity and uniformity of God's people, Jews and Gentiles alike. Essentially, the covenant promises of God apply to Israel and converted Gentiles.

In contrast, dispensation theology teaches that God's promises are dispensed through various revelations over time. This viewpoint doesn't necessarily discard the value of covenants and how they frame the relationship of humanity and God. However, dispensations augment covenants through revelations given by the prophets. Dispensations attempt to explain revelations and interpret how they tie into God's overall plan including the sequencing and timing of events and redemption through the Messiah's return.

Also, dispensationalists believe the church (made up of believing Christians) and Israel are separated when it comes to the fulfillment of prophecy. They believe that only Israel will go through the tribulation and restoration prophesied for the end times.

According to Charles Ryrie, formerly of Dallas Theological Seminary, you will be able to recognize dispensationalists if they believe in three essentials.[8]

- a consistent literal interpretation of scripture,
- distinguishing between God's plan for Israel and the church, and
- that the glory of God manifest in a multifaceted way is the goal of history.

Not all Christian theologians agree with dispensationalism, which is held primarily by some premillennials. However, this book will be neutral in this matter and not attempt to argue one viewpoint over another. Instead, it will simply provide the scriptures pertaining to the Messiah's return and outline current perspectives and interpretations of those verses.

Covenants Frame God's Plan for the Messiah's Return

To recap, what does all this have to do with prophesy and the return of the Messiah? Prophecy is history written in advance. Isaiah 46:10 says, "I make known the end from the beginning, from ancient times, what is still to come. I say, 'My purpose will stand, and I will do all that I please.'" Bible prophecy is God's infallible message to us spoken or written by prophets chosen by God. Also, prophecy is inspired by God. The apostle Peter wrote,

²⁰ Above all, you must understand that no prophecy of Scripture came about by the prophet's own interpretation of things. ²¹ For prophecy never had its origin in the human will, but prophets, though human, spoke from God as they were carried along by the Holy Spirit. (2 Peter 1:20-21)

In a sense, covenants are prophetic. Their contract with humanity and Israel span generations and foresee a time when God's purpose and promises are fulfilled. In *God's Kingdom through God's Covenants*, Peter Gentry wrote,

> It is primarily through the biblical covenants viewed across time that we learn how God's kingdom will arrive. This is why grasping the progression of the covenants is at the heart of understanding how God's kingdom dawns in Jesus, how God's redemptive promise is realized, and how the entire metanarrative of the Bible hangs together, since the biblical covenants constitute the framework and backbone for the entire storyline of Scripture.[9]

Essentially, every covenant points the way to Jesus and to restored fellowship with God, all of which will culminate with the Messiah's return as King.

In the remaining pages, we will see how the prophecies and signs are being fulfilled around us. Current events and turmoil in our world give every indication that we are in the end times and that it will likely not be long before the Lord returns in power and glory. This demands that as Christians, we wake up! We need to understand the signs of the times. We need to be ready as believers.

> Essentially, every covenant points the way to Jesus and to restored fellowship with God, all of which will culminate with the Messiah's return as King.

I'm reminded of when King David was at war and men were joining his army at Hebron. One group from Issachar was described in 1 Chronicles 12:32 as "men who understood the times and knew what Israel should do." When you consider the men of God who received the covenants from God, who were they? Only one was a king; the rest were ordinary men living in a sinful world who made a decision to believe God, to repent of their sins, and to live out that belief through obedience.

Christians are not on this earth to blend into the culture; we are here to be a light, a beacon to the future event that is sure to come and to serve God by sharing his holy message. We are born again to be relevant. We must understand the times and know what we should do just as the men from Issachar in the time of David.

In the following pages, we will see the signs that precede the Messiah's return and learn that our right response to those difficult times will brighten our light in a dark world and show others the way to salvation.

Bible Study Questions

Define the following.

1. **Providence** is the _____ of the Creator who is _____ involved in moving his creation to a goal.

2. **Eschatology** is what the Bible teaches about the _____.

3. A **Covenant** is an _____ commitment between God and his people.

What are the key points of the covenants of the Old Testament?

4. **Edenic (Creation) Covenant** (Genesis 1:28–30; 2:15–17)
   • Established _____ and relationship to humanity.
   • Man's responsibility toward _____.

5. **Adamic Covenant** (Genesis 3:14–19)
   • Initiated due to Adam's sin.
   • _____ state of humanity and creation.
   • God's _____ for that sin.

6. **Noahic Covenant** (Genesis 8:20–9:17)
   • Restated God's authority over humanity and its duties.
   • Added animosity between _____, allowed humanity to eat _____, punishment for _____.

7. **Abrahamic Covenant** (Genesis 15:4–21)
   • Father of a multitude of _____.
   • Geographical boundaries of the nation of _____.
   • _____ to the world through his seed

8. **8. Mosaic (Old; Mount Sinai) Covenant** (Deuteronomy 11:26–28).
   • Included Ten Commandments (Exodus 20:1–17) and over 600 commands (the Law).
   • _____ for obedience; _____ for disobedience.

9. **Palestinian (Land) Covenant** (Deuteronomy 30:1–10)
   • Expanded on Abrahamic covenant.
   • _____of Israel due to disobedience, _____, and eventual _____.

10. **Davidic Covenant** (2 Samuel 7:8–16)
   - Lineage would be _____.
   - Foundation for _____ promises.
   - His _____ would be on the throne and rule as king.

11. **New Covenant** (Jeremiah 31:31–34)
   - Future _____ of Israel.
   - Provides for the _____ of sins.
   - Universal _____ of the Lord.

12. **Prophecy** is _____ written in _____.

Reflection

The covenants in the Old Testament remind us that God is in control of our present and future. In what ways have you seen God's control in your life?

CHAPTER 2

SEVEN KEY MESSAGES FROM OLD TESTAMENT PROPHETS

Of the greatness of his government and peace there will
be no end. He will reign on David's throne and over
his kingdom, establishing and upholding it with justice
and righteousness from that time on and forever.
—Isaiah 9:7

Reading prophecies in the Old Testament regarding the end times and the end of the age can be challenging. Interpretations of these prophesies are somewhat augmented in the New Testament. As we read about the signs and Jesus's return, we benefit from Jesus and his disciples explaining many of the prophetic messages of the Old Testament, their meaning, and how they foreshadow his first and second coming.

Many of the prophecies in the Old Testament are directed toward God's chosen people. The events surrounding the Messiah's return are staged in the Holy Land. For example, the abomination that causes desolation stands in the temple of Jerusalem; when Jesus returns, his foot will rest on Mount Olivet and his millennium throne will be in Jerusalem.

Also, the prophets often use dual reference and prophetic perspective, which essentially blurs the timing of the events and references current and future occurrences. This can make interpretation of the scriptures difficult, and as a result, we see many diverse opinions about their meaning.

There are three common forms in which a prophecy may be delivered—symbolically, as an abbreviated vision for events that occur over a long period, or in reference to dual events.

First, a prophecy is often full of symbolism and imagery. Symbolism is recognizable when the prophet states that something appears like an item or when it is clear that a story is an analogy. In Jewish culture, certain places and things were also commonly used symbolically. For example, Babylon was symbolic of religious apostasy and olive oil of wealth and the spirit of God (Revelation 14:8, 18:2).

Second, a prophecy may also be written from a prophetic perspective in which there is an abbreviated or single vision but the events unfold over thousands of years. For example, the prophecies of the Messiah intermingle events relating to his first and second coming. It wasn't until the New Testament and revelation of Jesus as the fulfillment of Old Testament prophecies that it became clear there would be two events—a first coming as Savior and a subsequent return in power and glory.

A third approach is for the prophecy to have dual referencing where two or more events are involved. In this case, the fulfillment of the more immediate event confirms the accuracy and reliability of the prophet's vision and foreshadows the future event.

Thankfully, men and women have dedicated their lives to the study and interpretation of these scriptures, and we can benefit from their insights and efforts.

According to Anthony Hoekema, "Eschatology must not be thought of as something which is found only in, say, such Bible books as Daniel and Revelation, but as dominating and permeating the entire message of the Bible."[10] Hoekema outlined seven revelational concepts taught through the prophets of the Old Testament.

1. Coming Redeemer
2. Kingdom of God
3. New covenant

4. Restoration of Israel
5. Outpouring of the Spirit
6. Day of the Lord
7. New heavens and the new earth

With this framework in mind, let's begin looking at a few key prophecies in the Old Testament.

Coming Redeemer

There are five groups of prophecies related to the coming Redeemer. The first is that the Redeemer would be the seed of a woman, her offspring: "And I will put enmity between you and the woman, and between your offspring and hers; he will crush your head, and you will strike his heel" (Genesis 3:15). From the very beginning, the prophecy was that the Redeemer would defeat Satan, that "her offspring ... will crush [his] head." Also, the Messiah will be from the seed of Abraham (Genesis 22:18), a descendant of the tribe of Judah (Genesis 49:10) and of David (2 Samuel 7:12–13). God will establish his throne forever.

> And through your [Abraham's] offspring all nations and earth will be blessed. (Genesis 22:18)

> The scepter will not depart from Judah ... until he to whom it belongs shall come and the obedience of the nations shall be his. (Genesis 49:10)

> When your days are over and you rest with your ancestors, I will raise up your offspring to succeed you, your own flesh and blood, and I will establish his kingdom. He is the one who will build a house for my Name, and I will establish the throne of his kingdom forever. (2 Samuel 7:12–13)

Second, the Redeemer is recognized as having three offices—prophet, priest, and king. In Deuteronomy 18:15, Moses said, "The Lord your God will raise up for you a prophet like me from among you, from your fellow Israelites. You must listen to him." Zechariah prophesied, "See, your king comes to you, righteous and victorious, lowly and riding on a donkey, on a colt, the foal of a donkey" (Zechariah 9:9). And in Psalm 110:4, David said, "The Lord has sworn and will not change his mind: 'You are a priest forever, in the order of Melchizedek'."

> ¹ The Lord says to my lord: "Sit at my right hand until I make your enemies a footstool for your feet." ² The Lord will extend your mighty scepter from Zion, saying, "Rule in the midst of your enemies!" ³ Your troops will be willing on your day of battle. Arrayed in holy splendor, your young men will come to you like dew from the morning's womb. ⁴ The Lord has sworn and will not change his mind: "You are a priest forever, in the order of Melchizedek." ⁵ The Lord is at your right hand; he will crush kings on the day of his wrath. ⁶ He will judge the nations, heaping up the dead and crushing the rulers of the whole earth. ⁷ He will drink from a brook along the way, and so he will lift his head high. (Psalm 110:1–7)

Psalm 110 is one of the most quoted in the New Testament and pictures the Messiah as sharing the Father's kingly authority (vv. 1–2), as priest (v. 4), and as victorious warrior (vv. 5–7). Verses 5–6 state the Messiah would "crush kings on the day of his wrath" and would "judge nations." This day of wrath is widely understood to be the time of Jesus's return.

Another verse often used to discuss the Messiah is Isaiah 9:6–7. The Messiah will be known by many names referenced in this short and poignant outpouring of prophecy. He will be the "Wonderful (meaning 'supernatural') Counselor," "Mighty God," "Everlasting Father," and "Prince of Peace."

⁶ For to us a child is born, to us a son is given, and the government will be on his shoulders. And he will be called Wonderful Counselor, Mighty God, Everlasting Father, Prince of Peace. ⁷ Of the greatness of his government and peace there will be no end. He will reign on David's throne and over his kingdom, establishing and upholding it with justice and righteousness from that time on and forever. The zeal of the Lord Almighty will accomplish this. (Isaiah 9:6–7)

Third, we see the Messiah identifying with the coming of God to his people. Isaiah 7:14 reads, "The virgin will conceive and give birth to a son, and will call him Immanuel." In Hebrew, "Immanuel" means "God with us."

Fourth, the Messiah will be a suffering servant. Isaiah 53:5 reads, "He was pierced for our transgressions, he was crushed for our iniquities; the punishment that brought us peace was on him, and by his wounds we are healed."

And fifth, the Messiah is the Son of Man. In Daniel 7, Daniel recalled,

¹³ In my vision at night I looked, and there before me was one like a son of man, coming with the clouds of heaven. He approached the Ancient of Days [God the Father] and was led into his presence. ¹⁴ He was given authority, glory and sovereign power; all nations and peoples of every language worshiped him. His dominion is an everlasting dominion that will not pass away, and his kingdom is one that will never be destroyed. (Daniel 7:13-14)

In the New Testament, the Son of Man was clarified to be the Messiah (Matthew 1:16).

Kingdom of God

Though the term kingdom of God is not found in the Old Testament, the teaching that God is King is referenced in Psalms and the books of the prophets. Let's look at Psalm 47, where the Lord is clearly presented as the great king over all the earth.

> ¹ Clap your hands, all you nations; shout to God with cries of joy. ² For the Lᴏʀᴅ Most High is awesome, the great King over all the earth …⁷ For God is the King of all the earth; sing to him a psalm of praise. ⁸ God reigns over the nations; God is seated on his holy throne. (Psalm 47: 1–2, 7–8)

Daniel predicted that the messianic kingdom would be tied to the coming Redeemer. Daniel 2:44 reads, "In the time of those kings, the God of heaven will set up a kingdom that will never be destroyed, nor will it be left to another people. It will crush all those kingdoms and bring them to an end, but it will itself endure forever."

Also, Psalm 2 refers to Jesus's return and his rule in the millennium. During this time, God will establish his son as ruler and those who oppose him will be rebuked.

> ² The kings of the earth rise up and the rulers band together against the Lᴏʀᴅ and against his anointed, saying, ³ "Let us break their chains and throw off their shackles." ⁴ The One enthroned in heaven laughs; the Lord scoffs at them. ⁵ He rebukes them in his anger and terrifies them in his wrath, saying, ⁶ "I have installed my king on Zion, my holy mountain." (Psalm 2:2–6)

New Covenant

The new covenant may sound familiar since we discussed this in the first chapter. Though Jeremiah's prophecies are primarily those of doom, in the midst of them is good news—the promise of a new covenant.

> [31] "The days are coming," declares the LORD, "when I will make a new covenant with the people of Israel and with the people of Judah. [32] It will not be like the covenant I made with their ancestors when I took them by the hand to lead them out of Egypt, because they broke my covenant, though I was a husband to them," declares the LORD. [33] "This is the covenant I will make with the people of Israel after that time," declares the LORD. "I will put my law in their minds and write it on their hearts. I will be their God, and they will be my people. [34] No longer will they teach their neighbor, or say to one another, 'Know the LORD,' because they will all know me, from the least of them to the greatest," declares the LORD. "For I will forgive their wickedness and will remember their sins no more." (Jeremiah 31:31–34)

The key elements of this new covenant are that the Lord will put his "law in their minds and write it on their hearts" (v. 33), that he "will be their God and they will be my people" (v. 33), and that he will "forgive their wickedness and remember their sins no more" (v. 34).

In the New Testament, we see confirmation that the new covenant was fulfilled by Jesus Christ. Hebrews 8:6–13 clearly links Jesus to the new covenant as its mediator. "But in fact the ministry Jesus has received is as superior to theirs as the covenant of which he is mediator is superior to the old one" (Hebrews 8:6).

⁶ But in fact the ministry Jesus has received is as superior to theirs as the covenant of which he is mediator is superior to the old one, since the new covenant is established on better promises. ⁷ For if there had been nothing wrong with that first covenant, no place would have been sought for another. ⁸ But God found fault with the people and said: "The days are coming, declares the Lord, when I will make a new covenant with the people of Israel and with the people of Judah. ⁹ It will not be like the covenant I made with their ancestors when I took them by the hand to lead them out of Egypt, because they did not remain faithful to my covenant, and I turned away from them, declares the Lord. ¹⁰ This is the covenant I will establish with the people of Israel after that time, declares the Lord. I will put my laws in their minds and write them on their hearts. I will be their God, and they will be my people. ¹¹ No longer will they teach their neighbor, or say to one another, 'Know the Lord,' because they will all know me, from the least of them to the greatest. ¹² For I will forgive their wickedness and will remember their sins no more." ¹³ By calling this covenant "new," he has made the first one obsolete; and what is obsolete and outdated will soon disappear. (Hebrews 8:6–13)

The scriptures we quote each time we take communion (1 Corinthians 11:23–26) remind us that Jesus's sacrifice on the cross made possible the fulfillment of the new covenant. "This cup is the new covenant in my blood" (v. 25), says the Lord. We continue this ritual, proclaiming "the Lord's death until he comes" (v. 26), which is a direct reference to his return.

Restoration of Israel

The prophets predicted that Israel and Judah would be carried away into captivity by hostile nations and would be scattered (dispersed) as a result of their disobedience, idolatry, and apostasy. In the midst of judgment, we see prophecies of hope like the new covenant. Another ray of hope is the prophecy of restoration such as the one in Isaiah 11.

> [11] In that day the Lord will reach out his hand a second time to reclaim the surviving remnant of his people from Assyria, from Lower Egypt, from Upper Egypt, from Cush, from Elam, from Babylonia, from Hamath and from the islands of the Mediterranean. [12] He will raise a banner for the nations and gather the exiles of Israel; he will assemble the scattered people of Judah from the four quarters of the earth. (Isaiah 11:11–12)

The Lord will "reclaim the surviving remnant of his people" in that day (v. 11). He will "gather the exiles of Israel" and "assemble the scattered people of Judah" (v. 12).

Other verses that reference the dispersion and restoration of Israel are in Deuteronomy 4. Moses warned the Israelites, "If you then become corrupt and make any kind of idol ... doing evil in the eyes of the Lord ... the Lord will scatter you among the peoples" (Deuteronomy 4:25–27). However, if you repent and "seek the Lord ... return to the Lord your God and obey him" (Deuteronomy 4:29–30), you will find that the "Lord your god is a merciful God and he will not abandon or destroy you or forget the covenant with your ancestors" (Deuteronomy 4:31).

Though the restoration of Israel was not one of the signs Jesus called out on the Mount of Olives as preceding his return, it was prophesied in the Old Testament as an event that would occur in the day of the Lord. Many feel this prophecy began to be fulfilled with the reestablishment of Israel as a nation following World War II.

Outpouring of the Spirit

Another message taught in Old Testament prophecy is the outpouring of the Holy Spirit in Joel 2:28–29. As we approach the day of the Lord, the Spirit is poured out on God's servants.

> [28] And afterward, I will pour out my Spirit on all people. Your sons and daughters will prophesy, your old men will dream dreams, your young men will see visions. [29] Even on my servants, both men and women, I will pour out my Spirit in those days. [30] I will show wonders in the heavens and on the earth, blood and fire and billows of smoke. [31] The sun will be turned to darkness and the moon to blood before the coming of the great and dreadful day of the Lord. (Joel 2:28–31)

Next, Joel prophesied that there would be signs of heavenly upheaval. There will be "wonders in the heavens and on the earth, blood and fire and billows of smoke," including the sun "turned to darkness" and the "moon to blood," all of which would occur before the "coming of the great and dreadful day of the Lord" (Joel 2:30–31). We hear a lot about these signs today. It seems every time there is an eclipse of the sun or a blood moon, rumors swirl as to the timing of the return of Jesus. There is even a book whose title references this prophecy, *Four Blood Moons: Something is about to Change*, by John Hagee.

While we expect these signs to occur, we must remember no one knows the day or time of Jesus's return. At best, we can look at these events and know that as the intensity of heavenly events increase, his return draws nearer.

In the book of Joel, it would appear that what Joel saw as coming together in a single vision are actually events separated from each other by hundreds of years.

Day of the Lord

The phrase *day of the Lord* is used nineteen times in the Old Testament; it usually identifies events that take place at the end of time. However, it can also refer to a span of time during which God personally intervenes in history, directly or indirectly, to accomplish some specific aspect of his plan. Both the Greek and Hebrew words commonly used in this phrase, *hemera* and *yowm*, can be translated into the literal twenty-four-hour period of a day or be used figuratively as a period of time or an age.

In Obadiah 1:15, it refers to a day when God will bring swift destruction on Israel's enemies. "The day of the LORD is near for all nations. As you have done, it will be done to you; your deeds will return upon your own head." Or in Isaiah 13:9–11, it refers to a final and future day of judgment for evil: "See, the day of the LORD is coming—a cruel day, with wrath and fierce anger— to make the land desolate and destroy the sinners within it … I will punish the world for its evil, the wicked for their sins."

The day of the Lord can also refer to a day of wrath for Judah as found in Zephaniah 1:14–15. It becomes clear from the rest of Zephaniah that the day of wrath refers to both a day of judgment for Judah, as well as a final worldwide catastrophe.

> [14] The great day of the LORD is near—near and coming quickly. The cry on the day of the LORD is bitter; the Mighty Warrior shouts his battle cry. [15] That day will be a day of wrath—a day of distress and anguish, a day of trouble and ruin, a day of darkness and gloom, a day of clouds and blackness—[16] a day of trumpet and battle cry against the fortified cities and against the corner towers. (Zephaniah 1:14–16)

Other references to the day of wrath are in Amos and Isiah. Amos warned, "Woe to you who long for the day of the Lord! … That day will be darkness, not light" (Amos 5:18). Isaiah pointed out the just reward for those who oppose the Lord.

> The LORD Almighty has a day in store for all the proud and lofty, for all that is exalted (and they will be humbled) … The arrogance of man will be brought low and human pride humbled; the LORD alone will be exalted in that day, and the idols will totally disappear. (Isaiah 2:12, 17–18)

And finally, the day of the Lord can refer to salvation for those who call on the name of the Lord. Joel 2:32 reads, "Everyone who calls on the name of the LORD will be saved; for on Mount Zion and in Jerusalem there will be deliverance, as the LORD has said, even among the survivors whom the LORD calls."

Some scholars associate the day of the Lord with a "special day that will occur when God's will and purpose for his world and for mankind are fulfilled." Others believe the day of the Lord will be a "longer period of time than a single day—a period of time when Christ will reign throughout the world before he cleanses heaven and earth in preparation for the eternal state of all mankind." Still others believe it refers to an "instantaneous event when Christ returns to earth to redeem his faithful believers and send unbelievers to eternal damnation."[11] One theme consistent to all of these interpretations is that this is a time when the Lord will be victorious once and for all over evil.

New Heavens and New Earth

When the Messiah returns and humanity is restored to a life of obedience and righteousness, the earth will also be restored. Recall that in Genesis 3, the fall of humanity resulted in the earth being cursed.

> [17] To Adam he said, "Because you listened to your wife and ate fruit from the tree about which I commanded

you, 'You must not eat from it.' Cursed is the ground because of you; through painful toil you will eat food from it all the days of your life. [18] It will produce thorns and thistles for you, and you will eat the plants of the field." (Genesis 3:17–18)

A number of verses in Isaiah point to a restored and new heavens and earth. Peace and harmony between animals and humanity was prophesied (Isaiah 11:6–8). More important, there is a restored relationship with the Lord as the earth is described as "filled with the knowledge of the Lord" (Isaiah 11:9).

[6] The wolf will live with the lamb, the leopard will lie down with the goat, the calf and the lion and the yearling together; and a little child will lead them. [7] The cow will feed with the bear, their young will lie down together, and the lion will eat straw like the ox. [8] The infant will play near the cobra's den, and the young child will put its hand into the viper's nest. [9] They will neither harm nor destroy on all my holy mountain, for the earth will be filled with the knowledge of the LORD as the waters cover the sea. (Isaiah 11:6–9)

Later in Isaiah 35, the curse on the ground will be lifted and there will be restoration of the land so even the driest areas will have springs of water and the desert will blossom (Isaiah 35:2, 6). Humanity will be healed from all illness and physical deformities (Isaiah 35:5–6).

[1] The desert and the parched land will be glad; the wilderness will rejoice and blossom. Like the crocus, [2] it will burst into bloom; it will rejoice greatly and shout for joy. The glory of Lebanon will be given to it, the splendor of Carmel and Sharon; they will see the glory of the LORD, the splendor of our God. [3] Strengthen the feeble hands, steady the knees that give way; [4] say to

those with fearful hearts, "Be strong, do not fear; your God will come, he will come with vengeance; with divine retribution he will come to save you." ⁵ Then will the eyes of the blind be opened and the ears of the deaf unstopped. ⁶ Then will the lame leap like a deer, and the mute tongue shout for joy. Water will gush forth in the wilderness and streams in the desert. ⁷ The burning sand will become a pool, the thirsty ground bubbling springs. In the haunts where jackals once lay, grass and reeds and papyrus will grow. ⁸ And a highway will be there; it will be called the Way of Holiness; it will be for those who walk on that Way. The unclean will not journey on it; wicked fools will not go about on it. ⁹ No lion will be there, nor any ravenous beast; they will not be found there. But only the redeemed will walk there, ¹⁰ and those the LORD has rescued will return. They will enter Zion with singing; everlasting joy will crown their heads. Gladness and joy will overtake them, and sorrow and sighing will flee away. (Isaiah 35:1–10)

Finally, in Isaiah, we are told new heavens and a new earth will be created. Once again, peace, prosperity, well-being, abundant crops, and fellowship with the Lord will be the defining trademark of these times.

¹⁷ See, I will create new heavens and a new earth. The former things will not be remembered, nor will they come to mind. ¹⁸ But be glad and rejoice forever in what I will create, for I will create Jerusalem to be a delight and its people a joy. ¹⁹ I will rejoice over Jerusalem and take delight in my people; the sound of weeping and of crying will be heard in it no more. ²⁰ Never again will there be in it an infant who lives but a few days, or an old man who does not live out his years; the one who dies at a hundred will be thought a mere child; the one who fails to reach a hundred will be considered accursed.

²¹ They will build houses and dwell in them; they will plant vineyards and eat their fruit. ²² No longer will they build houses and others live in them, or plant and others eat. For as the days of a tree, so will be the days of my people; my chosen ones will long enjoy the work of their hands. ²³ They will not labor in vain, nor will they bear children doomed to misfortune; for they will be a people blessed by the LORD, they and their descendants with them. ²⁴ Before they call I will answer; while they are still speaking I will hear. (Isaiah 65:17–24)

The focus of the Old Testament prophesies is the path from the original sin in Genesis to the final restoration of God's chosen people to himself.

These seven themes in the Old Testament confirm the coming of the Redeemer, the establishment of his eternal kingdom, the judgment of the ungodly, and the restoration of the earth and those called to be God's children. Whereas the focus of the signs of the end times discussed in the New Testament was preparing God's people for the time between his ascension and return, the focus of the Old Testament prophesies is the path from the original sin in Genesis to the final restoration of God's chosen people to himself. What a truly remarkable God who has shown such love and forgiveness toward humanity!

Bible Study Questions

There are seven key revelation messages related to the future from the Old Testament.

1. **Coming Redeemer/Messiah**
   a. Seed of woman and Abraham; descendant of Abraham, tribe of Judah and David; God will establish his throne _____.
   b. Prophet, priest, king—kings will be crushed on the _____; He will _____ the nations.
   c. God coming to his people—Immanuel.
   d. Suffering servant.
   e. Son of Man—Messiah will come with the clouds; given _____ and sovereign _____; _____ dominion.

2. **Kingdom of God**—Lord is the great _____ over all the earth.

3. **New covenant**—The Lord will put his _____ in their minds and write it on their hearts; will be their _____, and they will be my _____; He will _____ their wickedness and remember their sins no more.

4. **Restoration of Israel**—In that day the Lord will reclaim a surviving _____, gather the _____ of Israel, and assemble the _____ of Judah.

5. **Outpouring of the Spirit**—In those days, I will pour out my _____ on my servants.

6. **Day of the Lord**—_____ of Israel's enemies; day of _____; day of _____.

7. **New heaven and new earth**—Peace in animal world; Full of _____ of the Lord; Desert shall _____; springs of water.

Reflection

As you consider the world stage today, which Old Testament prophecies do you think have been fulfilled? Which ones haven't been fulfilled yet?

CHAPTER 3

DANIEL'S VISION OF FUTURE KINGDOMS

Lord, listen! Lord, forgive! Lord, hear and act! For your sake, my God,
do not delay, because your city and your people bear your Name.
—Daniel 9:19

The book of Daniel prophesies about the kingdoms that will control
Israel and precede the coming of the Messiah. It begins during the
reign of Jehoiakim, king of Judah, when the land was defeated by the
Babylonians, when Daniel was about fifteen. Along with approximately
a hundred other select young men, Daniel was taken from his home and
family in Jerusalem and became a part of those exiled to Babylon. He
was of noble descent, "without any physical defect, handsome, showing
aptitude for every kind of learning, well informed, quick to understand,
and qualified to serve in the king's palace" (Daniel 1:4)—the very
qualities that Nebuchadnezzar was looking for in his palace servants.

Babylon was in what is now Iraq. Today, this area is primarily ruins,
but during Daniel's lifetime, it had fifty-six miles of impenetrable walls
framing some two hundred square miles of state-of-the-art dwellings,
teeming entertainment centers, thriving businesses, at least three palaces,
and extravagant temples to numerous gods.[12] To put this in perspective,
two hundred square miles is about half the size of New York City.

Daniel 1 established the character of Daniel as a man determined
to follow God and remain true to Him. When the king provided the

young men from Judah portions from his table, Daniel along with his three friends decided not to defile themselves by eating them. Many of the dietary restrictions for Israel are listed in Leviticus 11. For example, they would be defiled if they ate pork, shrimp, shellfish, and many types of seafood, most insects, scavenger birds, and various other animals.

Daniel requested permission from the chief official to change his diet, and at the end of ten days, "they looked healthier and better nourished than any of the young men who ate the royal food" (Daniel 1:15). Unfortunately, the other young men who had traveled to Babylon with Daniel did not feel as strongly about their principles, and it showed!

Because of their obedience, God gave knowledge and understanding to these four young men. In addition, he gave Daniel the ability to understand visions and dreams.

There are three dreams recorded in Daniel—one dreamt by the king Nebuchadnezzar and two by Daniel. These dreams have similar interpretation in that they all concern future kingdoms leading up to the Messianic kingdom ruled by the Lord. But before we look at the detailed interpretation of the dreams, let's first quickly review the three dreams.

Nebuchadnezzar's Dream of a Statue

The first dream occurred just as Daniel was finishing his three-year training program in preparation to serve the king. Nebuchadnezzar had a troubling dream and demanded his "magicians, enchanters, sorcerers and astrologers" to reveal both the dream and its interpretation (Daniel 2:2). None of the king's court could meet this demand, so the king's verdict was to kill them all. Daniel stepped up and volunteered to provide the interpretation. After a sleepless night of prayer, Daniel received from God the details and interpretation of the dream. Imagine Daniel's faith to believe that God would hear and answer his prayer in such a way. Keep in mind that Daniel was probably just seventeen or eighteen at the time.

> Imagine Daniel's faith to believe that God would hear and answer his prayer in such a way.

In the dream, the king saw an enormous, dazzling statue made of different materials: "The head of the statue was made of pure gold, its chest and arms of silver, its belly and thighs of bronze, its legs of iron, its feet partly of iron and partly of baked clay" (Daniel 2:32–33). And finally, apart from the statue was a rock cut out of a mountain that demolished the statue.

> 34 While you were watching, a rock was cut out, but not by human hands. It struck the statue on its feet of iron and clay and smashed them. 35 Then the iron, the clay, the bronze, the silver and the gold were all broken to pieces and became like chaff on a threshing floor in the summer. The wind swept them away without leaving a trace. But the rock that struck the statue became a huge mountain and filled the whole earth. (Daniel 2:34–35)

From head to toe, each part of the statue appeared to be separate in material content yet somehow connected and interdependent by being symbolized as a body. In the first four kingdoms that had already emerged, the territorial domain of each kingdom overlapped somewhat and were in the Mediterranean and the Middle East. Each subsequent kingdom was larger than the prior one, and all exercised control over Israel. The final two kingdoms prophesied have not occurred yet.

Daniel's Dream of Four Beasts Emerging from the Sea

Many years went by before Daniel had a second dream. A lot happened to Daniel and his friends. Over and over, Daniel's resolve and faith were tested. In Daniel 3, Daniel's friends refused to worship the image of Nebuchadnezzar. Bravely, they told the king,

> If we are thrown into the blazing furnace, the God we
> serve is able to deliver us from it, and he will deliver us
> from Your Majesty's hand. But even if he does not, we
> want you to know, Your Majesty, that we will not serve
> your gods or worship the image of gold you have set up.
> (Daniel 3:17–18)

The king promptly threw them into the furnace. Fortunately, God stepped in and supernaturally delivered them from the fire.

In Daniel 4, Nebuchadnezzar lost his mind and lived like an animal for seven years. At the end of this time, God restored him for a brief period before he died. In Daniel 5, a new king, Belshazzar, was crowned; he was a descendant of Nebuchadnezzar. Belshazzar was corrupt and defiled items from the Jerusalem temple. At a huge drunken gathering of his governors and other leaders, God passed judgment on Belshazzar. Suddenly, a hand appeared and wrote on the wall, "Mene, Mene, Tekel, Parsin" (Daniel 5:25).

> Here is what these words mean: Mene: God has
> numbered the days of your reign and brought it to an
> end. Tekel: You have been weighed on the scales and
> found wanting. Peres: Your kingdom is divided and
> given to the Medes and Persians. (Daniel 5:26–28)

Later that evening, Belshazzar was killed by Darius, and the second kingdom, the one led by the Medo-Persians and Cyrus the Great, emerged.

Soon afterward, Daniel was tested again. A law was passed forbidding the worship of any god other than Darius (Daniel 6:7). Since Daniel was committed to praying three times a day to the one true God of Israel, he was quickly brought before the king for judgment and condemned to die. He was thrown into the lion's den from which God miraculously delivered him. At that point, it should have been obvious that God had had a plan for Daniel, one in which supernatural intervention played a big role. It should give us great comfort to know that humans cannot thwart or stop God's plans.

As we get to Daniel 7, Daniel was around sixty-seven or sixty-eight; over forty-five years had passed. In this setting, Daniel was faced with another dream. This time, it was his.

> [1] In the first year of Belshazzar king of Babylon, Daniel had a dream, and visions passed through his mind as he was lying in bed. He wrote down the substance of his dream. [2] Daniel said: "In my vision at night I looked, and there before me were the four winds of heaven churning up the great sea. [3] Four great beasts, each different from the others, came up out of the sea. [4] The first was like a lion, and it had the wings of an eagle. I watched until its wings were torn off and it was lifted from the ground so that it stood on two feet like a human being, and the mind of a human was given to it. [5] And there before me was a second beast, which looked like a bear. It was raised up on one of its sides, and it had three ribs in its mouth between its teeth. It was told, 'Get up and eat your fill of flesh!' [6] After that, I looked, and there before me was another beast, one that looked like a leopard. And on its back it had four wings like those of a bird. This beast had four heads, and it was given authority to rule. [7] After that, in my vision at night I looked, and there before me was a fourth beast—terrifying and frightening and very powerful. It had large iron teeth; it crushed and devoured its victims and trampled underfoot whatever was left. It was different from all the former beasts, and it had ten horns." (Daniel 7:1–7)

In his dream, Daniel saw four beasts come from the sea; the "sea" was symbolic of a time of turmoil. The first beast was a lion with wings like an eagle (v. 4), the second was a bear with three ribs in its mouth

(v. 5), the third was a leopard with four wings and four heads (v. 6), and the fourth was a beast with large iron teeth and ten horns (v. 7).

We will see later that these animals and their characteristics parallel the interpretation of the dream of the statue in Daniel 2 and represent kingdoms. But before we delve into the details of the kingdoms, let's continue with a quick look at the remaining dream.

Daniel's Dream of a Ram and Goat

Daniel had a second dream regarding the kingdoms of the Medo-Persians and Greeks in Daniel 8. This dream occurred approximately three years after the dream of the four beasts emerging from the sea. At that time, Daniel was an old man around seventy. Once again, animals were used symbolically to represent kingdoms—a ram (v. 3) and a goat (v. 5).

> [1] In the third year of King Belshazzar's reign, I, Daniel, had a vision, after the one that had already appeared to me. [2] In my vision I saw myself in the citadel of Susa in the province of Elam; in the vision I was beside the Ulai Canal. [3] I looked up, and there before me was a ram with two horns, standing beside the canal, and the horns were long. One of the horns was longer than the other but grew up later. [4] I watched the ram as it charged toward the west and the north and the south. No animal could stand against it, and none could rescue from its power. It did as it pleased and became great. [5] As I was thinking about this, suddenly a goat with a prominent horn between its eyes came from the west, crossing the whole earth without touching the ground. [6] It came toward the two-horned ram I had seen standing beside the canal and charged at it in great rage. [7] I saw it attack the ram furiously, striking the ram and shattering its two horns. [8] The goat became very great, but at the

height of its power the large horn was broken off, and in its place four prominent horns grew up toward the four winds of heaven. (Daniel 8:1–8)

These dreams have similarities; they all reference the same kingdoms as becomes evident by the interpretations given to Daniel. They predict that four major kingdoms will have control and power over Israel and the territories surrounding it—the Babylonian, Medo-Persian, Greek, and Roman. After a period, a fifth kingdom will emerge prior to the culmination of the Messiah's return and establishment of his kingdom on earth.

Babylonian Kingdom

The first kingdom prophesied in Nebuchadnezzar's and Daniel's dreams was the Babylonian kingdom represented by the head of gold in Nebuchadnezzar's dream of the statue (Daniel 2:32). Daniel interpreted the head to represent Nebuchadnezzar (Daniel 2:38) and the kingdom of Babylon.

> [32] The head of the statue was made of pure gold ... [37] Your Majesty, you are the king of kings. The God of heaven has given you dominion and power and might and glory; [38] in your hands he has placed all mankind and the beasts of the field and the birds in the sky. Wherever they live, he has made you ruler over them all. You are that head of gold. (Daniel 2: 32, 37–38)

In Daniel's dream of the four beasts, the first to emerge from the sea was a lion with "wings of an eagle" and the "mind of a human" (Daniel 7:4). Given Nebuchadnezzar's brief bout with insanity and behaving like a wild animal in Daniel 4, this may explain the emphasis of a human mind. This beast represented the Babylonian Empire.

The Babylonian Empire led by Nebuchadnezzar, his predecessor

Nabopolassar, and briefly by his descendants was in power from 626 to 539 BC and was later defeated by the Medo-Persians.[13] The boundaries of the Babylonian Empire reached as far north to Cilicia, south to Egypt and Arabia, west to Cyprus and the Mediterranean coastal cities, and east to Media and Persia.[14] To put the reign of this empire in perspective of Daniel's life, Daniel and his friends were taken from Jerusalem in 605 BC. Daniel lived until the third year of the reign of Cyrus, which would have been around 536 BC.[15]

In summary, the Babylonian kingdom was

- represented by head of pure gold (Daniel 2:32),
- represented by lion with eagle wings (Daniel 7:4),
- history: its king was Nebuchadnezzar (Daniel 2:38).

Medo-Persian Kingdom

The next kingdom prophesied in Nebuchadnezzar and Daniel's dreams was the Medo-Persian kingdom represented by the chest and arms of silver in Nebuchadnezzar's dream of the statue (Daniel 2:32) and would be inferior to Babylon: "Its chest and arms of silver … After you, another kingdom will arise, inferior to yours" (Daniel 2:32, 39).

In Daniel's dream of the four beasts, the second to emerge from the sea was a lopsided bear with three ribs in its mouth (Daniel 7:5). The bear was told to "get up and eat your fill of flesh" (Daniel 7:5), which meant to expand and conquer new areas. The Medo-Persian kingdom led by Cyrus the Great made "three major conquests—Babylon (539 BC), Lydia (546 BC), and Egypt (525 BC)."[16]

In Daniel's second dream of the ram and the goat, Gabriel told Daniel, "The two-horned ram that you saw represents the kings of Media and Persia" (Daniel 8:20). Note that the ram had two horns and one was longer that the other. Initially, the empire was ruled jointly by the kings of Media and Persia. But later, the Persian Empire prevailed and Cyrus the Great established the Achaemenid Empire "encompassing around 8 million square kilometers across three continents, making it the largest empire in the ancient world."[17]

In addition to the prophecies we see in Daniel regarding this kingdom, Isaiah and Jeremiah also foretold its ascension in power. Isaiah quoted God as saying, "See, I will stir up against them the Medes … their bows will strike down the young men" (Isaiah 13:17–18). Jeremiah prophesied that the Medes would expand beyond Babylonia. He warned to "prepare the nations for battle against her—the kings of the Medes, their governors and all their officials, and all the countries they rule" (Jeremiah 51:28).

God used the Medo-Persian ascendancy "to destroy Babylon and take vengeance for [God's] temple" (Jeremiah 51:11). Shortly after the Persians defeat of Babylon in 539 BC, God also moved the heart of Cyrus to allow the Jews to return to Judah.

The Medo-Persian Empire existed from around 538 BC to 333 BC[18] and was later defeated by Alexander the Great, the leader of the Greek Empire.

In summary, the Medo-Persian Empire

- was represented by chest and arms of silver (Daniel 2:32),
- was represented by bear with three ribs in its mouth (Daniel 7:5),
- was represented by two-horned ram (Daniel 8:3),
- would arise after Babylon and be inferior (Daniel 2:39),
- would be defeated by the goat (Daniel 8:7),
- history: king was Cyrus the Great; three major conquests were made by this kingdom—Babylon, Lydia, and Egypt.

Greek Kingdom

The third kingdom prophesied in Nebuchadnezzar and Daniel's dreams was the Greek kingdom represented by the belly and thighs of bronze in Nebuchadnezzar's dream of the statue (Daniel 2:32) and was prophesied to be strong and rule over the whole earth (Daniel 2:39).

In Daniel's dream of the four beasts, the third to emerge from the sea was a leopard with four wings and four heads (Daniel 7:6). The third kingdom was "given authority to rule" (Daniel 7:6). Note that this was very similar to what we read in Daniel 2:39, that this kingdom would "rule over the whole earth."

The prophecy regarding this kingdom was that "four kings will rise" (Daniel 7:17) but that ultimately, "the holy people of the Most High will receive the kingdom" (Daniel 7:18). This encouragement of Israel's ultimate victory would be needed during some very rough times that would come less than four hundred years after the lifetime of Daniel.

In Daniel's second dream of the ram and the goat, the "shaggy goat is the king of Greece," and the "large horn between its eyes is the first king" (Daniel 8:21) was Alexander the Great. Alexander died unexpectedly at the height of his power (Daniel 8:8) from a high fever. The "four horns" (Daniel 8:8, 22) that grew up in his place were the four generals who divided his empire and ruled after his death. Cassander ruled Macedonia and Greece, Lysimachus ruled Thrace and parts of Asia Minor, Ptolemy ruled Egypt and parts of Asia Minor, and Seleucus ruled Syria, Israel, and Mesopotamia.

> [21] The shaggy goat is the king of Greece, and the large horn between its eyes is the first king. [22] The four horns that replaced the one that was broken off represent four kingdoms that will emerge from his nation but will not have the same power. (Daniel 8:21–22)

From the four horns emerged another leader referenced as "another horn" (v. 9). This leader was a descendant of Seleucus, Antiochus Epiphanes, who ruled 175–164 BC. His short reign typified the intense cruelty and ungodliness that will characterize the "man of lawlessness" in the end times. In particular, Antiochus Epiphanes set himself against the people of God; he actively took steps to break down their worship. He "took away the daily sacrifice" for the Lord, tore down his sanctuary, and trampled "underfoot the Lord's people" (Daniel 8:11, 13). The prophecy indicated that the surrender of the sanctuary would last 2,300 days (Daniel 8:14), or a little over six years.

> [9] Out of one of them came another horn, which started small but grew in power to the south and to the east and toward the Beautiful Land. [10] It grew until it reached the host of the heavens, and it threw some of the starry host down to the earth and trampled on them. [11] It set itself up to be as great as the commander of the army of the LORD; it took away the daily sacrifice from the LORD, and his sanctuary was thrown down. [12] Because of rebellion, the LORD's people and the daily sacrifice were given over to it. It prospered in everything it did, and truth was thrown to the ground. (Daniel 8:9–12)

The Greek Empire existed from 333 BC to 63 BC[19] and was later defeated by the Roman Empire. At its greatest extent, the Greek empire included the entire ruins of the Persian Empire: modern territories of Iran, Turkey, parts of Central Asia, Pakistan, Thrace and Macedonia, much of the Black Sea coastal regions, Afghanistan, Iraq, northern Saudi Arabia, Jordan, Israel, Lebanon, Syria, and all significant population centers of ancient Egypt as far west as Libya.[20]

In summary, the Greek kingdom

- was represented by belly and thighs of bronze (Daniel 2:32),
- was represented by leopard with four wings and four heads (Daniel 7:6),
- was represented by shaggy goat and four horns (Daniel 8:21–22), and
- would rule over whole earth (Daniel 2:39),
- kingdom was given authority to rule (Daniel 7:6),
- at the height of its power, the large horn was broken off and four prominent horns grew and took its place (Daniel 8:8, 22),

- history: king was Alexander the Great; four generals who ruled after his death were Cassander, Lysimachus, Ptolemy, and Seleucus.

Roman Kingdom

The fourth kingdom prophesied in Nebuchadnezzar and Daniel's dreams was the Roman Empire represented by the legs of iron in Nebuchadnezzar's dream of the statue (Daniel 2:33) and would be strong as iron and would crush and break the others (Daniel 2:40).

In Daniel's dream of the four beasts, the fourth to emerge from the sea was a beast with large iron teeth and ten horns (Daniel 7:7). The fourth kingdom, which was terrifying and powerful, "crushed and devoured its victims and trampled underfoot what was left" (Daniel 7:19). This was also similar to the fourth kingdom in Daniel 2, which was said to "crush and break the others" (Daniel 2:40).

While the interpretation of the dream does not provide the name of the kingdom, the first Roman emperor ruled in 27 BC, and the Western Roman Empire fell in AD 476. The Eastern Roman Empire endured longer but fell in 1453 to the Ottoman Turks. This empire had numerous leaders. Some of those well-known in the first century of the empire were the first emperor Octavian (Augustus), who ruled from 27 BC to AD 14, Tiberius, who ruled from AD 14 to 37, and Nero, who ruled from 54 to 68.[21] The Roman Empire was in power during the life of Jesus and the time of the early church; it actively persecuted the followers of Jesus.

The territory of the Roman Empire extended as far north as the "British Channel," the "Rhine" and "Danube" rivers and "the Black Sea." It extended south to the "deserts of Africa, the cataracts of the Nile, and the Arabian deserts." It extended as far east as "the Euphrates" and as far west as "the Atlantic."[22] Essentially, the kingdom included nations on all sides of the Mediterranean.

It is significant to note that the kingdoms in Daniel's dream focus on the future of Israel. It is not that the other nations of the earth have disappeared but rather that they are out of focus as we look at kingdoms impacting God's chosen people.

In summary, the Roman kingdom

- was represented by legs of iron (Daniel 2:33),
- was represented by beast with large iron teeth (Daniel 7:7),
- was represented by little horn (Daniel 8:9),
- would crush and break the others (Daniel 2:40),
- was terrifying and very powerful; it crushed and devoured its victims; it had ten horns (Daniel 7:7),
- history: Most notable rulers were Octavian (Augustus), Tiberius, and Nero.

Ten-Kingdom Confederacy

The fifth kingdom prophesied in Nebuchadnezzar's and Daniel's dreams occurred in the future as the time for Christ's return nears. This kingdom is represented by feet partly of iron and partly of baked clay in Nebuchadnezzar's dream of the statue (Daniel 2:33). It will be a divided kingdom "partly strong and partly brittle, and will not remain united" (Daniel 2:41–43).

> [33] Its feet partly of iron and partly of baked clay ... [41] Just as you saw that the feet and toes were partly of baked clay and partly of iron, so this will be a divided kingdom; yet it will have some of the strength of iron in it, even as you saw iron mixed with clay. [42] As the toes were partly iron and partly clay, so this kingdom will be partly strong and partly brittle. [43] And just as you saw the iron mixed with baked clay, so the people will be a mixture and will not remain united, any more than iron mixes with clay. (Daniel 2:33, 41–43)

In Daniel's dream of the four beasts, a fifth kingdom emerged from the fourth beast with ten horns (Daniel 7:7). From this kingdom, a little horn will come up from among them and begin to rule (Daniel 7:8). This divided kingdom is made up of ten kings who will come from the kingdom of the beast (the Roman Empire). The leader who will rise up among them will be "boastful" (Daniel 7:8).

> [7] After that, in my vision at night I looked, and there before me was a fourth beast … It was different from all the former beasts, and it had ten horns. [8] While I was thinking about the horns, there before me was another horn, a little one, which came up among them; and three of the first horns were uprooted before it. This horn had eyes like the eyes of a human being and a mouth that spoke boastfully. (Daniel 7:7–8)

In Daniel 9:9, the scene shifts to events in heaven. God the Father is being described in verses 9–10. He destroys the little horn but allows the other leaders to live for a time.

> [9] As I looked, thrones were set in place, and the Ancient of Days took his seat. His clothing was as white as snow; the hair of his head was white like wool. His throne was flaming with fire, and its wheels were all ablaze. [10] A river of fire was flowing, coming out from before him. Thousands upon thousands attended him; ten thousand times ten thousand stood before him. The court was seated, and the books were opened. [11] Then I continued to watch because of the boastful words the horn was speaking. I kept looking until the beast was slain and its body destroyed and thrown into the blazing fire. [12] The other beasts had been stripped of their authority, but were allowed to live for a period of time. (Daniel 7:9–12)

Because there are ten kingdoms represented by the ten horns, the fifth kingdom is known as the ten-kingdom confederacy. A leader will emerge in this kingdom who will subdue three of the kings and wage "war against the holy people." This ruler has many names—the Antichrist (1 John 2:18), the abomination that causes desolation (Matthew 24:15) and the man of lawlessness (2 Thessalonians 2:3). These references point to his ungodly character and foreshadow the destruction and evil his kingdom will foster. He will "speak against the Most High" and will try to "change the set times and laws."

> [20] I also wanted to know about the ten horns on its head and about the other horn that came up, before which three of them fell—the horn that looked more imposing than the others and that had eyes and a mouth that spoke boastfully. [21] As I watched, this horn was waging war against the holy people and defeating them, [22] until the Ancient of Days came and pronounced judgment in favor of the holy people of the Most High, and the time came when they possessed the kingdom … [24] The ten horns are ten kings who will come from this kingdom. After them another king will arise, different from the earlier ones; he will subdue three kings. [25] He will speak against the Most High and oppress his holy people and try to change the set times and the laws. The holy people will be delivered into his hands for a time, times and half a time. (Daniel 7:20–25)

Daniel 7:25 indicates that the little horn will prevail over God's holy people "for a time, times and half a time." This is usually interpreted to mean three and a half years based on the timeline given in Revelation 13:5–7 of forty-two months.

> [5] The beast was given a mouth to utter proud words and blasphemies and to exercise its authority for forty-two months. [6] It opened its mouth to blaspheme God, and to slander his name and his dwelling place and those

who live in heaven. [7] It was given power to wage war against God's holy people and to conquer them. And it was given authority over every tribe, people, language and nation. (Revelation 13:5–7)

Others look at Daniel 4:25 to understand the duration of a time when Daniel prophesied that the king would remain in an animal state for a period of seven times, which equated to seven years. So a "time, times and a half" would be three and a half years.

You will be driven away from people and will live with the wild animals; you will eat grass like the ox and be drenched with the dew of heaven. Seven times will pass by for you until you acknowledge that the Most High is sovereign over all kingdoms on earth and gives them to anyone he wishes. (Daniel 4:25)

In Daniel's second dream of the ram and the goat, while the fifth kingdom in not directly referenced, we are told starting in Daniel 8:23 that the prophecy that follows pertains to the end times. Similar to the little horn referenced in Daniel 7, a "master of intrigue" will rise up during the time of the end, become strong, and seek to "destroy the holy people" (Daniel 8:24).

[17] As he came near the place where I was standing, I was terrified and fell prostrate. "Son of man," he said to me, "understand that the vision concerns the time of the end." [18] While he was speaking to me, I was in a deep sleep, with my face to the ground. Then he touched me and raised me to my feet. [19] He said: "I am going to tell you what will happen later in the time of wrath, because the vision concerns the appointed time of the end … [23] In the latter part of their reign, when rebels have become completely wicked, a fierce-looking king, a master of intrigue, will arise. [24] He will become

very strong, but not by his own power. He will cause astounding devastation and will succeed in whatever he does. He will destroy those who are mighty, the holy people. [25] He will cause deceit to prosper, and he will consider himself superior. When they feel secure, he will destroy many and take his stand against the Prince of princes. Yet he will be destroyed, but not by human power. [26] The vision of the evenings and mornings that has been given you is true, but seal up the vision, for it concerns the distant future." (Daniel 8:17–19, 23–26)

The ten-kingdom confederacy will be the final kingdom preceding the return of Jesus. Just as the first four kingdoms encompassed Israel, we expect this kingdom to as well. In fact, since the ten horns emerge out of the beast, this kingdom will likely find its roots in the nations that encompassed the Roman Empire. The evil leader and the ten kings of this confederacy will wage war against the Lamb, but the Lamb will "triumph over them" (Revelation 17:12).

[12] The ten horns you saw are ten kings who have not yet received a kingdom, but who for one hour will receive authority as kings along with the beast. [13] They have one purpose and will give their power and authority to the beast. [14] They will wage war against the Lamb, but the Lamb will triumph over them because he is Lord of lords and King of kings—and with him will be his called, chosen and faithful followers. (Revelation 17:12–14)

While we don't know the exact time of the emergence of this kingdom, it is separated from the previous four kingdoms by a significant time gap. The last kingdom we saw was the Roman Empire, which existed before, during, and after the life of Jesus. Both this kingdom and the next one, the Messianic kingdom, are yet to come. This gap in emergence of the kingdoms will be discussed further when we get to the dream of the seventy-sevens.

In summary, the ten-kingdom confederacy

- was represented by feet of iron and mixed clay (Daniel 2:33),
- was represented by beast with ten horns; ; three horns uprooted (Daniel 7:7–8); these represent ten kings who will come from kingdom of the beast (Daniel 7:24),
- will be divided; partly strong and partly brittle; will not remain united (Daniel 2:41–43),
- little horn rose up from among them—boastful (Daniel 7:8); will subdue three kings (Daniel 7:24); will wage war against the holy people (Daniel 7:21); will speak against the Most High (Daniel 7:25, 9:24); will try to change set times and law; will prevail three and a half years (Daniel 7:25); will take away daily sacrifice and sanctuary surrendered (Daniel 8:11); will be destroyed but not by human power (Daniel 5:25),
- vision concerns the appointed time of the end (Daniel 8:19), and
- future ruler: Antichrist (foreshadowed by Antiochus Epiphanes)

Messianic Kingdom

The sixth and final kingdom prophesied in Nebuchadnezzar and Daniel's dreams will occur in the future and is the Messianic kingdom. This kingdom is represented by a rock divinely cut out that will demolish the statue (Daniel 2:34). This kingdom will crush all the other kingdoms and endure forever (Daniel 2:44).

> [34] While you were watching, a rock was cut out, but not by human hands. It struck the statue on its feet of iron and clay and smashed them. [35] Then the iron, the clay, the bronze, the silver and the gold were all broken to pieces and became like chaff on a threshing floor in the summer. The wind swept them away without leaving a

trace. But the rock that struck the statue became a huge mountain and filled the whole earth … [44] In the time of those kings, the God of heaven will set up a kingdom that will never be destroyed, nor will it be left to another people. It will crush all those kingdoms and bring them to an end, but it will itself endure forever. [45] This is the meaning of the vision of the rock cut out of a mountain, but not by human hands—a rock that broke the iron, the bronze, the clay, the silver and the gold to pieces. The great God has shown the king what will take place in the future. The dream is true and its interpretation is trustworthy. (Daniel 2:34–35, 44–45)

In Daniel's dream of the four beasts, the sixth kingdom is represented by one like the Son of Man coming with the clouds of heaven (Daniel 7:13). This may sound familiar. In Acts 1:11, as the apostles watched Jesus ascend into the clouds, the angelic beings confirmed that Jesus, "who has been taken from you into heaven, will come back in the same way you have seen him go into heaven." The Son of Man will also be "given authority, glory and sovereign power" and he will be worshiped by "all nations" (Daniel 7:14). Finally, he will have an "everlasting dominion" that will "not pass away" or be "destroyed" (Daniel 7:14). His kingdom will represent victory for the holy people of God and will be "everlasting."

[13] In my vision at night I looked, and there before me was one like a son of man, coming with the clouds of heaven. He approached the Ancient of Days and was led into his presence. [14] He was given authority, glory and sovereign power; all nations and peoples of every language worshiped him. His dominion is an everlasting dominion that will not pass away, and his kingdom is one that will never be destroyed … [26] But the court will sit, and his power will be taken away and completely destroyed forever. [27] Then the sovereignty,

power and greatness of all the kingdoms under heaven will be handed over to the holy people of the Most High. His kingdom will be an everlasting kingdom, and all rulers will worship and obey him. (Daniel 7:13–14, 26–27)

In summary, the Messianic kingdom

- was represented by rock cut out of mountain (Daniel 2:34),
- was represented by Son of Man (Daniel 7:13),
- will crush all other kingdoms; kingdom will never be destroyed and will endure forever (Daniel 2:44),
- Son of Man will come with clouds of heaven; given authority, glory and sovereign power; worshiped by all nations; (Daniel 7:13); will have everlasting dominion (Daniel 7:27), and
- future ruler: Messiah

Seventy Sevens: A Timeline Given by God

In Daniel 9, we find Daniel in deep prayer for his people. "Daniel understood from the Scriptures, according to the word of the Lord given to Jeremiah the prophet, that the desolation of Jerusalem would last seventy years" (Daniel 9:2).

Daniel was a man of faith. He believed the prophecies about the nation of Israel. Jeremiah, a prophet who had lived before and in the early years of Daniel, had prophesied that the captivity by Babylon would last seventy years (Jeremiah 25:11).

> [8] Therefore the LORD Almighty says this: "Because you have not listened to my words, [9] I will summon all the peoples of the north and my servant Nebuchadnezzar king of Babylon," declares the LORD, "and I will bring them against this land and its inhabitants and against all the surrounding nations. I will completely destroy them

and make them an object of horror and scorn, and an everlasting ruin. ¹⁰ I will banish from them the sounds of joy and gladness, the voices of bride and bridegroom, the sound of millstones and the light of the lamp. ¹¹ This whole country will become a desolate wasteland, and these nations will serve the king of Babylon seventy years." (Jeremiah 25:8–11)

Since it had almost been seventy years since the exile of the Jews to Babylon, Daniel began praying and petitioning God on behalf of his people. Daniel acknowledged the sin of the people of Judah and that their exile and captivity at that time was the result. In Daniel 9:7, he confessed, "Lord, you are righteous, but this day we are covered with shame—the people of Judah and the inhabitants of Jerusalem and all Israel, both near and far, in all the countries where you have scattered us because of our unfaithfulness to you." This confession starts in verse 5 and continues through verse 14. As Daniel came to the end of the prayer, he asked God to forgive Israel's sin. In Daniel 9:19, he besought God, "Lord, listen! Lord, forgive! Lord, hear and act! For your sake, my God, do not delay, because your city and your people bear your Name."

In the midst of his prayer, Daniel received a surprise revelation from the angel Gabriel. He received a timeline for when God would deliver his people from Babylonian captivity and for eternity. This portion of scripture is where we get the seventy sevens timeline and refers to the timeline "to bring in everlasting righteousness," or the Messianic kingdom (Daniel 9:24).

²⁰ While I was speaking and praying, confessing my sin and the sin of my people Israel and making my request to the LORD my God for his holy hill— ²¹ while I was still in prayer, Gabriel, the man I had seen in the earlier vision, came to me in swift flight about the time of the evening sacrifice. ²² He instructed me and said to me, "Daniel, I have now come to give you insight and understanding. ²³ As soon as you began to pray, a

word went out, which I have come to tell you, for you are highly esteemed. Therefore, consider the word and understand the vision: ²⁴ Seventy 'sevens' are decreed for your people and your holy city to finish transgression, to put an end to sin, to atone for wickedness, to bring in everlasting righteousness, to seal up vision and prophecy and to anoint the Most Holy Place." (Daniel 9:20–24)

The interpretation of these verses is a much-debated topic. Some do not take this timeline literally. However, given the context in which this verse occurs—that is, during the literal fulfillment of the seventy-year exile to Babylon, it is probable that this timeline should be taken literally as well. Also, there is much discussion as to when the seventy sevens time periods will occur. Many believe that this time is not consecutive but rather references that three periods of time are separated by other periods, that part of this time has passed, and that part of the time remains.

"Seventy 'sevens' are decreed for your people and your holy city" (Daniel 9:24). The verb *decreed* comes from the Hebrew word *chathak*. This is the only place in the Old Testament where this word is used, and it is translated as "cut off," "decide," and "determine." In other words, God had "cut off" a certain period of time from the remainder of history for a specific purpose. Also, note that this period of time has been set apart specifically for Daniel's people, who would be the Jews, and the "holy city," which would be Jerusalem.

Second, in verse 24, we see the purpose of this time period. During it, six things will be accomplished— "to finish transgression, to put an end to sin, to atone for wickedness, to bring in everlasting righteousness, to seal up vision and prophecy, and to anoint the Most Holy Place." The first three items accomplished relate to atoning for sin and cleansing Israel. To "finish transgression" refers to ending the apostasy of the Jews. To "put an end to sin" may mean either to atone for sin or to seal up sin in the sense of judging it finally. To "atone for wickedness" refers to the death of Christ on the cross, which is the basis for Israel's future forgiveness. "And in this way all Israel will be saved. As it is written:

'The deliverer will come from Zion; he will turn godlessness away from Jacob. [27] And this is my covenant with them when I take away their sins'" (Romans 11:26–27).

The last three items accomplished relate to the establishment of the millennial kingdom with the Messiah ruling. To "bring in everlasting righteousness" refers to the advent of the millennial kingdom of the Messiah.

> "The days are coming," declares the Lord, "when I will raise up for David a righteous Branch, a King who will reign wisely and do what is just and right in the land. In his days Judah will be saved and Israel will live in safety. This is the name by which he will be called: The Lord our Righteous Savior'" (Jeremiah 23:5–6).

To "seal up vision and prophecy" is to set God's seal of fulfillment on all the prophecies concerning the Jewish people and Jerusalem. And finally, to "anoint the Most Holy Place" is to anoint the millennial temple.

The seventy sevens are broken out as follows. Keep in mind that Jewish years are based on a 360-day year, not a 365-day year. Each set of sevens equates to seven years. To get the full length of the period, you multiply the number of sevens times seven. Below is a summary of the time periods we will be looking at.

- first time period—seven sevens equals 49 years
- second time period—sixty-two sevens equals 434 years
- third time period—one seven equals 7 years

First Time Period—Rebuilding Jerusalem

The first time period referenced is the time when the word goes out "to restore and rebuild Jerusalem" (Daniel 9:25). We are also told that the temple will be rebuilt in times of trouble, which is exactly what happened; the temple was built with opposition from neighboring tribes and took longer than it might have otherwise.

> Know and understand this: From the time the word goes out to restore and rebuild Jerusalem ... there will be seven "sevens," ... It will be rebuilt with streets and a trench, but in times of trouble. (Daniel 9:25)

Starting with verse 25, we see reference to when the word goes out to restore and rebuild Jerusalem. Shortly after ascending to the throne, Cyrus, the ruler of the Medo-Persian Empire, was led by God to free the Jews from captivity. The seventy-year period prophesied by Jeremiah had been fulfilled! But Cyrus did not stop there; he also authorized the rebuilding of the temple (2 Chronicles 36:22–23) in 444 BC.

> [22] In the first year of Cyrus king of Persia, in order to fulfill the word of the LORD spoken by Jeremiah, the LORD moved the heart of Cyrus king of Persia to make a proclamation throughout his realm and also to put it in writing: [23] This is what Cyrus king of Persia says: "The LORD, the God of heaven, has given me all the kingdoms of the earth and he has appointed me to build a temple for him at Jerusalem in Judah. Any of his people among you may go up, and may the LORD their God be with them." (2 Chronicles 36:22–23)

In addition to releasing the Jews, Cyrus returned the stolen temple articles and paid for the Jews' rebuilding efforts from the royal treasury (Ezra 6:3–5).

Shortly thereafter, the Persian ruler Artaxerxes Longimanus gave Nehemiah permission to restore and rebuild Jerusalem (Nehemiah 2:1, 5, 8). "This was a monumental time in Israel's history, as Jerusalem and the temple were rebuilt and the Law was reinstituted."[23]

> [1] In the month of Nisan in the twentieth year of King
> Artaxerxes … [5] If it pleases the king and if your servant
> has found favor in his sight, let him send me to the city
> in Judah where my ancestors are buried so that I can
> rebuild it … [8] the king granted my requests. (Nehemiah
> 2:1, 5, 8)

There were several decrees issued during this period related to the rebuilding of the temple, thus making it difficult to establish an exact start date for calculating the length of time between the decree and the completion of the temple. However, this second rebuilding of the temple was completed in 396 BC, approximately forty-nine Jewish years after the decree by Cyrus.

Math check:

1) How long is seven sevens? 7 x 7 = 49 Jewish years.
2) Based on the Jewish calendar, how long is 49 years? 49 years x 360 days/year = 17,640 days.
3) Convert 49 Jewish years to the Roman calendar: 17,640 days ÷ 365 days/year = 48.3 years.
4) Confirm the time span: 444 BC–396 BC—approximately 48 Roman years.

Second Time Period—Advent of the Anointed One

The second time period referenced is sixty-two sevens in addition to the seven sevens from when the word goes out "to restore and rebuild Jerusalem" until the "Anointed One will be put to death" (Daniel 9:25–26).

> [25] Know and understand this: From the time the word
> goes out to restore and rebuild Jerusalem until the
> Anointed One, the ruler, comes, there will be seven
> "sevens," and sixty-two "sevens." … [26] After the sixty-two

"sevens," the Anointed One will be put to death and will
have nothing. (Daniel 9:25–26)

In Luke 22, we see that Jesus was crucified in the month of Nisan.
This scripture referenced Jesus's last supper with his disciples, which
occurred during the celebration of Passover just days prior to his death.
Passover is celebrated during the Hebrew month of Nisan, which is
around March. (Note that in Western countries, Passover is celebrated
in early- to mid-April and is always close to Easter.)

Based on the time of the rule of Pontius Pilate (AD 26–36), scholars
estimate the timing of Jesus's crucifixion to be either AD 30 or 33
depending on the start and duration of Jesus's ministry. There are
arguments supporting both dates, but this book assumes the later date.
Regardless, the early church believed Jesus was the Anointed One and
that he fulfilled the prophecies of the Old Testament, which are often
quoted in the writings of the apostles and letters of Paul.

Math check:

1) How long is sixty-two sevens? 62 x 7 = 434 Jewish years.
2) Based on the Jewish calendar, how long is 434 years in addition
   to the 49 years to rebuild the temple? 434 + 49 years = 483 years,
   and 483 years x 360 days/year = 173,880 days.
3) Convert 483 Jewish years to the Roman calendar: 173,880 days
   ÷ 365 days/year = 476.2 years.
4) Confirm the time span: 444 BC—AD 33 = 477 less 1 year for
   conversion from BC to AD, which is approximately 476 Roman
   years.

Third Time Period—Tribulation
Preceding the Millennial Kingdom

Finally, it's from Daniel 9 that we get the seven-year tribulation
period. Since the first two periods were fulfilled literally, the seventieth
seven could be expected to be fulfilled literally as well. The last 7

years are separated from the first 483 years. After the Anointed One is put to death, he "will have nothing." Then the "end will come as a flood" (Daniel 9:26). In verse 26, "nothing" can be interpreted as an unspecified period of time.

> [26] After the sixty-two "sevens," the Anointed One will be put to death and will have nothing. The people of the ruler who will come will destroy the city and the sanctuary. The end will come like a flood: War will continue until the end, and desolations have been decreed. [27] He will confirm a covenant with many for one "seven." In the middle of the "seven" he will put an end to sacrifice and offering. And at the temple he will set up an abomination that causes desolation, until the end that is decreed is poured out on him. (Daniel 9:26–27)

In verse 27, the one who will "confirm a covenant with many" is understood to be a ruler in the final seven years before the Messiah returns. We are told that in the middle of the seven-year period, "he will put an end to sacrifice and offering" and "set up an abomination that causes desolation" (Daniel 9:27). Because this time will be a horrible time for God's people, it is often referred to as the tribulation period. Later, we are told in Daniel that from "the time that the daily sacrifice is abolished and the abomination that causes desolation is set up, there will be 1,290 days" (Daniel 12:11). One thousand two hundred and ninety days is approximately three and a half years. The prophecy that the "end will come like a flood" is consistent with New Testament teachings that the return of the Messiah will be sudden and unexpected (Daniel 9:26).

In the math check below, you may notice that the fourth step—the confirmation of the time span by using historical dates—is missing. Since this time period has not occurred yet, it cannot be validated yet as fulfilling the prophecy of lasting seven years. But instead, we assume its validity based on the fulfillment of the previous two time periods.

Math check:

1) How long is one seven? 1 x 7 = 7 Jewish years.
2) Based on the Jewish calendar, how long is 7 years? 7 years x 360 days/year = 2,520 days.
3) Convert 483 Jewish years to the Roman calendar: 2,520 days ÷ 365 days/year = 6.9 Roman years.

Daniel 9: Groups of Seven		
7 x 7 = 49 years	62 x 7 = 434 years	1 x 7 = 7 years
444 BC–396 BC	444 BC–AD 33	Future
(9:25) Time to restore and rebuild Jerusalem	(9:25-26) Time until the Anointed One put to death	(9:27) He will confirm a covenant with many; set up an abomination of desolation in temple (Daniel 12:11) From time daily sacrifice is abolished until abomination that causes desolation is set up, there will be 1,290 days

Exhibit 1: Seventy Sevens: A Timeline Given by God

God's Sovereignty over Kingdoms, Time, and Events

The book of Daniel reminds us that God is sovereign over time, events, and even empires and their leaders. In Daniel 2:20–21, we read, "Praise be to the name of God for ever and ever; wisdom and power are His. He changes times and seasons; He deposes kings and raises up others. He gives wisdom to the wise and knowledge to the discerning."

As we review the six empires in Daniel's prophecies, we see that four kingdoms have already passed and that two remain—the ten-kingdom confederacy and the Messianic kingdom. Just as the first four empires focused on the nation of Israel, we can expect the remaining two will also encompass Israel.

> By knowing these events before they happen, we can find courage and peace in the knowledge of God's sovereignty and promise of eternal resurrection for those who trust him.

We know that the fifth kingdom, the ten-kingdom confederacy led by the Antichrist, will be one of great distress for God's holy ones. By knowing these events before they happen, we can find courage and peace in the knowledge of God's sovereignty and promise of eternal resurrection for those who trust him.

Daniel 12:1–3 offers a word of hope in the days preceding the Messianic kingdom. Take a minute to read these verses below and offer a prayer of thanks to the almighty God who makes all this possible.

> [1] At that time Michael, the great prince who protects your people, will arise. There will be a time of distress such as has not happened from the beginning of nations until then. But at that time your people—everyone whose name is found written in the book—will be delivered. [2] Multitudes who sleep in the dust of the earth will awake: some to everlasting life, others to shame and everlasting contempt. [3] Those who are wise will shine like the brightness of the heavens, and those who lead many to righteousness, like the stars for ever and ever. (Daniel 12:1–3)

Bible Study Questions

1. **Daniel 2—Nebuchadnezzar's Dream**
List the items that the statue is made up of.

    a. head of _____
    b. chest and arms of _____
    c. belly and thighs of _____
    d. legs of _____
    e. feet of iron and _____
    f. _____ cut out of mountain

2. **Daniel 7—Dream of Four Beasts Emerging from the Sea**
List the beasts that emerge from the sea.

    a. _____ with eagle wings; mind of human
    b. lopsided _____ with three ribs in its mouth
    c. _____ with four wings and four heads
    d. _____ with large iron teeth and ten horns

3. **Daniel 8—Dream of Ram and Goat**
List the animals in Daniel's dream.

    a. Two-horned _____—kingdom of Medes and Persians
    b. _____ with prominent horn; broken off and replaced by four horns

4. **Babylonian kingdom**—represented by head of pure gold and lion; king is _____

5. **Medo-Persian kingdom**—represented by chest and arms of silver, bear and two-horned ram; will rise after Babylon and be _____; makes three major conquests

69

6. **Greek kingdom**—represented by belly and thighs of bronze, leopard, and shaggy goat; will rule over whole _____; prominent leader will be replaced by _____ less powerful generals

7. **Roman kingdom**—represented by legs of iron and beast w/ large iron teeth; will _____ and break the others; terrifying and very powerful; _____ and devoured its victims

8. **Ten-Confederacy kingdom**—represented by feet of iron and baked clay and ten horns of the Beast (Monster); _____ kingdom; partly strong and partly brittle; _____ rose up from among them—boastful; will subdue three _____; wages war against the _____ people; speaks against the Most High; tries to change set _____ and _____; prevails three and a half years

9. **Messianic kingdom**—represented by a rock and _____; will _____ all other kingdoms; will never be destroyed and will endure _____; Son of Man will come with clouds of heaven; given authority, glory and sovereign power; worshiped by all nations; everlasting _____

10. **Seventy Sevens**

    a. 1st through 7th groups of seven = 49 years—time to _____ and _____ Jerusalem
    b. 8th through 69th groups of seven = 434 years—time until the _____ put to death
    c. 70th group of seven = 7 years—time when "he" will confirm a covenant with many and set up an _____ that causes _____ in temple; 1,290 days from time daily sacrifice is abolished until abomination of desolation setup

Reflection

Daniel was a man of fervent prayer and understanding of scripture. As the time draws near for the people of God to be delivered from Babylon, Daniel prayed for their repentance and for God's forgiveness (Daniel 9:1–19). As we draw near to Jesus's return, what should we pray for God's people (Israel) and for believers worldwide?

CHAPTER 4

OTHER PROPHETIC VISIONS

Concerning this salvation, the prophets, who spoke of the grace
that was to come to you, searched intently and with the greatest
care, trying to find out the time and circumstances to which
the Spirit of Christ in them was pointing when he predicted the
sufferings of the Messiah and the glories that would follow.
—1 Peter 1:10–11

Daniel did not stand alone in prophesying the end times. Some other
key prophecies that related to the events of the end times and return
of the Messiah are those of Joel, Isaiah, Micah, Zephaniah, Ezekiel,
Zechariah, and Malachi.

Throughout the Old Testament are sprinklings of prophecy
regarding the terrible day of judgment, the restoration of Israel, and
the hope of a restored earth and godly people living in submission to
God. Through the various Old Testament prophecies, we see that God
has a plan that remains the same from the beginning to the end of
time. These prophecies assure us that the promises of God's covenants
will be fulfilled. They lay out additional insights and details that will
occur along the way, thus giving us milestones by which to watch the
progression of fulfillment.

The prophecies highlighted in this chapter are in order of the
dates they were given to the prophets, from oldest (835 BC) to most

recent (between 450 and 400 BC). And "most recent" refers to the last prophecy in the Bible before the time of Jesus. The prophecies of Daniel we looked at in the previous chapter fell somewhere in the middle of this group; they occurred between 603 and 536 BC.

Joel—Military Campaigns and Heavenly Upheaval

The book of Joel was written between 835 and 830 BC. Not much is known about Joel except that he was the son of Pethuel (Joel 1:1). Joel's prophecy was written during the days of King Joash, who was under the regency of the priests when he ascended the throne of Judah at age seven in 835 BC. King Joash's reign was characterized by material prosperity and social evils.

Given the prosperity of the time, it would be a normal human response for the people to neglect God and be consumed with comfort and pleasure. During times of plenty, people often forget and take for granted the true source of the very things they are enjoying. And the people of Judah did just that. They had begun to live sinful and immoral lives and neglected to worship and thank the true God.

In this time of plenty, Joel called the people of Judah to repentance and warned them and their neighbors of a future time when God would judge them. The most frequently referenced of Joel's prophecies regarding the end times are the invasion of locusts, which foreshadows a military invasion in the end times, the outpouring of the Holy Spirit, heavenly upheaval in the day of the Lord, and a reference to the final battle.

First, Joel prophesied a severe drought and an invasion of locusts, a harbinger of a future military campaign in the day of the Lord. This invasion comes as a result of the sins of God's people. In Joel 2:2, "a large and mighty army comes." "Nothing escapes" (Joel 2:3) this army, and "every face turns pale at the sight of them" (Joel 2:6). "They rush upon the city; they run along the wall. They climb into the houses; like thieves they enter through the windows" (Joel 2:9).

[1] The day of the LORD is coming. It is close at hand— [2] a day of darkness and gloom, a day of clouds and blackness. Like dawn spreading across the mountains a large and mighty army comes, such as never was in ancient times nor ever will be in ages to come. [3] Before them fire devours, behind them a flame blazes. Before them the land is like the garden of Eden, behind them, a desert waste— nothing escapes them. [4] They have the appearance of horses; they gallop along like cavalry. [5] With a noise like that of chariots they leap over the mountaintops, like a crackling fire consuming stubble, like a mighty army drawn up for battle.

[6] At the sight of them, nations are in anguish; every face turns pale. [7] They charge like warriors; they scale walls like soldiers. They all march in line, not swerving from their course. [8] They do not jostle each other; each marches straight ahead. They plunge through defenses without breaking ranks. They rush upon the city; they run along the wall. They climb into the houses; like thieves they enter through the windows. [10] Before them the earth shakes, the heavens tremble, the sun and moon are darkened, and the stars no longer shine. [11] The LORD thunders at the head of his army; his forces are beyond number, and mighty is the army that obeys his command. The day of the LORD is great; it is dreadful. Who can endure it? (Joel 2:1–11)

Next, as we approach the day of the Lord, the Spirit is poured out on God's servants. As a result, "your sons and daughters will prophecy, your old men will dream dreams, your young men will see visions" (Joel 2:28). Since God's Holy Spirit was poured out on believers on the day of Pentecost and has indwelled every believer since, this section can be interpreted as having already occurred or that in the final days, the

Spirit's filling will increase in intensity to offset the increasing presence of evil and persecution of the saints.

Joel prophesied that there would be signs of heavenly upheaval, "wonders in the heavens and on the earth, blood and fire and billows of smoke," including the sun "turned to darkness" and the "moon to blood," all of which would occur before the "coming of the great and dreadful day of the Lord" (Joel 2:30–31). While we can't assume that every blood moon and solar eclipses is the one preceding the Messiah's return, we can be sure that these celestial events will occur on the day of the Lord.

Joel also spoke of the restoration of Israel. In Joel 3:1–3, we read that God will "restore the fortunes of Judah and Jerusalem" and judge the nations for their actions against his people.

And finally, Joel prophesied a second battle in which "fighting men draw near" and farm tools are used as weapons (Joel 3:9–14). One possible interpretation is that this could be referring to the battle of Armageddon. In this interpretation, the sequence of events would be that the millennium reign, the thousand-year reign of the Messiah, will occur after Jesus returns. At the end of the millennium, Satan will be released one final time. Those who still resist obedience and wholehearted commitment to the Lord will gather for a final battle against God's people.

In this context, it would make sense that there would not be any weapons like those seen prior to the millennium since during the millennium, there will be an extended period of peace. People will take whatever they have and convert it to weapons. "Beat your plowshares into swords and your pruning hooks into spears" (Joel 3:10).

Joel warned them of a terrible day of judgment. As he called his people to repentance, he spoke the truth: "Multitudes, multitudes in the valley of decision! For the day of the LORD is near in the valley of decision" (Joel 3:14). We all will face judgment before God; our choices and decisions matter.

From Joel's prophesies, we know there will be terrible and destructive wars in the end times. Though there will be judgment, ultimately, Israel will repent and be restored. The Holy Spirit will be poured out on God's people and the kingdom of the Messiah will prevail.

Isaiah—Millennium and Beyond

The prophecies of Isaiah were written between 739 and 686 BC. "Born into an influential, upper-class family, Isaiah rubbed shoulders with royalty and gave advice concerning the foreign affairs of the nation."[24] The prophet Isaiah preached primarily a message of judgment and salvation. He was concerned with the political alliances Judah was making with foreign nations. The Israelites would be tempted to trust in their power and military might instead of God's power and might to protect Judah, and they may be influenced by foreign gods and teachings. He warned them of the consequences of sin and disobedience to God. He exhorted Judah and its kings to seek God and trust him alone.

Isaiah prophesied many events concerning the end times, but the best known are his references to judgment, the restoration of Israel, the defeat of Babylon and Egypt, the future millennial kingdom, and eventually the emergence of the new heavens and earth.

Starting in Isaiah 2, the people of God were warned that the "arrogance of man will be brought low and human pride humbled; the LORD alone will be exalted in that day, and the idols will totally disappear" (Isaiah 2:17–18). God will not share his sovereignty and holiness. In Exodus 20, the Ten Commandments begin with, "You shall have no other gods before me" (Exodus 20:3). This command includes physical idols fashioned by us as well as the idols in our hearts—money, knowledge, power, and so forth.

Also, Isaiah warned that God "will punish the world for its evil, the wicked for their sins" (Isaiah 13:11). There are many periods of judgment and repentance that Israel has gone through historically. Each time there is a period of sin, repentance, a short period of prosperity, a return to sin, and further consequence.

Despite Israel's disobedience, God is faithful and restoration is promised in Isaiah. "In that day the Lord will reach out his hand a second time to reclaim the surviving remnant of his people" (Isaiah 11:11). God will remember the covenants he's made with Abraham, David, and others. In modern times, we can already see God's hand at work in bringing a remnant of his people back to Israel. "Over the centuries many middle-eastern Jews migrated to Europe, America, Russia, and other countries to escape the persecution of Islam. Beginning in this century, however, dispersed Jews from all over the world have flocked to Israel."[25]

> [10] In that day the Root of Jesse will stand as a banner for the peoples; the nations will rally to him, and his resting place will be glorious. [11] In that day the Lord will reach out his hand a second time to reclaim the surviving remnant of his people from Assyria, from Lower Egypt, from Upper Egypt, from Cush, from Elam, from Babylonia, from Hamath and from the islands of the Mediterranean. [12] He will raise a banner for the nations and gather the exiles of Israel; he will assemble the scattered people of Judah from the four quarters of the earth. (Isaiah 11:10–12)

Next, Isaiah prophesied that Babylon and Egypt would be destroyed.

> Babylon, the glory of kingdoms, the beauty of the Chaldees' excellency, shall be as when God overthrew Sodom and Gomorrah. It shall never be inhabited, neither shall it be dwelt in from generation to generation: neither shall the Arabian pitch tent there; neither shall the shepherds make their fold there. (Isaiah 13:19–20)

Later, regarding Egypt, he prophesied, "And the LORD shall smite Egypt: he shall smite and heal it: and they shall return even to the LORD, and he shall be intreated of them, and shall heal them" (Isaiah 19:22).

Despite Egypt's sins and judgment at the hands of Judah, eventually the fear of God would spread to Egypt and they would repent.

The promise of restoration of God's people extends to his full creation, and we see the restoration of harmony to animals and the earth during the millennial reign of the Messiah.

> [6] The wolf will live with the lamb, the leopard will lie down with the goat, the calf and the lion and the yearling together; and a little child will lead them. [7] The cow will feed with the bear, their young will lie down together, and the lion will eat straw like the ox. [8] The infant will play near the cobra's den, and the young child will put its hand into the viper's nest. [9] They will neither harm nor destroy on all my holy mountain, for the earth will be filled with the knowledge of the Lord as the waters cover the sea. (Isaiah 11:6–9)

Later in Isaiah, restoration of the earth and healing of the people was foreseen.

> [1] The desert and the parched land will be glad; the wilderness will rejoice and blossom … [5] Then will the eyes of the blind be opened and the ears of the deaf unstopped. [6] Then will the lame leap like a deer, and the mute tongue shout for joy. Water will gush f forth in the wilderness and streams in the desert. (Isaiah 35:1, 5–6).

This beautiful picture of complete healing, health, and fruitfulness is a testament to God's restorative ability. God is able to overcome the brokenness in this world and in us. He is able to make everything new again.

Finally, Isaiah's vision takes him to the end of time, where he sees a new heaven and earth. "See, I will create new heavens and a new earth. The former things will not be remembered, nor will they come to mind" (Isaiah 65:17).

Isaiah's prophecies are delivered over many years, and his writings do not appear to be sequential. However, through Isaiah's visions, God warns his people about the consequences of sin while encouraging them with promises of eventual and total restoration. God's promise and covenants with his people will be fulfilled and cannot be thwarted.

Micah—Lord's Temple

Micah was a less influential prophet who lived during the times of Isaiah. Whereas Isaiah prophesied to the court in Jerusalem, "Micah, a Judean from Moresheth in the [southwest] of Palestine, preached to the common people of Judah."[26] His prophecies were recorded approximately 735–700 BC.

Micah warned the people that God would destroy Samaria, the capital of Israel, and that Judah would fall if the people did not stop sinning. Under the rule of King Jotham, the idols in the high places had not been removed from the kingdom (Micah 1:7). Though King Jotham overall recognized God, he did not purge his kingdom of those things, in this case idols, that would tempt his people to sin and turn away from God. I see a similarity here to today. While as a people we worship God, in the same breath, we tolerate sin in our nation. This simply doesn't work. As the psalmist reminds us, "Blessed is the one who does not walk in step with the wicked or stand in the way that sinners take or sit in the company of mockers" (Psalm 1:1).

While judgment would come if the people continued down a path of sin, Joel also prophesied that eventually there would be repentance, redemption, and forgiveness. Like many other prophets, Micah foresaw the return of a remnant of Israel and repentance. "I will surely gather all of you, Jacob; I will surely bring together the remnant of Israel" (Micah 2:12).

Micah 4 describes the future restoration of Israel and is generally understood to refer to the times of the millennium. During this time, "the law will go out from Zion and the word of the Lord from Jerusalem" (Micah 4:2). With and end to all wars (Micah 4:3) and the onset of peace, their weapons will be beaten into farming tools; they will no longer be needed.

> [1] In the last days the mountain of the LORD's temple will be established as the highest of the mountains; it will be exalted above the hills, and peoples will stream to it. [2] Many nations will come and say, "Come, let us go up to the mountain of the LORD, to the temple of the God of Jacob. He will teach us his ways, so that we may walk in his paths." The law will go out from Zion, the word of the LORD from Jerusalem. [3] He will judge between many peoples and will settle disputes for strong nations far and wide. They will beat their swords into plowshares and their spears into pruning hooks. Nation will not take up sword against nation, nor will they train for war anymore. [4] Everyone will sit under their own vine and under their own fig tree, and no one will make them afraid, for the LORD Almighty has spoken. [5] All the nations may walk in the name of their gods, but we will walk in the name of the LORD our God for ever and ever. (Micah 4:1–5)

Isn't it interesting to contrast this section with Joel 3? In Micah 4, weapons were converted to farm tools. In Joel 3, farm tools were converted to weapons.

In the millennium period foreseen by Micah, the Messiah will return in power to this world and will be established as king and rule during this time. His reign will be characterized by order, obedience to God, peace, and restoration.

Zephaniah—Day of Judgment

The prophecy of Zephaniah was recorded around 625 BC. Zephaniah was of noble birth in the lineage of his great-great-grandfather King

Hezekiah (Zephaniah 1:1) and helped prepare Judah for the revival that took place under King Josiah in 621 BC. "For more than half a century, times had been evil under kings Manasseh and Amon, and Zephaniah called his people to repentance."[27]

Zephaniah warned Judah that judgment was inevitable if they did not repent. "The great day of the Lord is near—near and coming quickly … That day will be a day of wrath" (Zephaniah 1:14–15). Judah be punished, and in the day of the Lord, the heathen nations would be destroyed by God.

> "Therefore wait for me," declares the LORD, "for the day I will stand up to testify. I have decided to assemble the nations, to gather the kingdoms and to pour out my wrath on them—all my fierce anger. The whole world will be consumed by the fire of my jealous anger." (Zephaniah 3:8)

Zephaniah prophesied a remnant in Israel would survive and God would restore and redeem Israel.

> "They will do no wrong; they will tell no lies. A deceitful tongue will not be found in their mouths. They will eat and lie down and no one will make them afraid … At that time I will gather you; at that time I will bring you home. I will give you honor and praise among all the peoples of the earth when I restore your fortunes before your very eyes," says the Lord. (Zephaniah 3:13, 20).

Repentance and restoration was a repeated theme of the prophets. When falling into sin and in need of forgiveness, the message was one of God's faithfulness. When repenting and turning back to God, the message was one of hope and mercy. While the consequence of humanity's sin would be judgment, despite the sin of the people, God would be faithful to keep his covenants. When humanity repented and turned back to God, he lovingly forgave them and restored them to fellowship and a relation with him.

When falling into sin and in need of forgiveness, the message was one of God's faithfulness. When repenting and turning back to God, the message was one of hope and mercy.

Ezekiel—Overthrow of Gog

Ezekiel recorded his prophecies between 593 and 573 BC during the time Daniel was in Babylon. He was from a priestly family and spent his early years in Jerusalem until he was taken by Nebuchadnezzar to Babylon in 597. Unlike Daniel, he was not from the royal family and therefore was not selected to serve in the palace. He settled near the river Kebar (Nebuchadnezzar's royal canal) and prophesied to the Babylonian exiles for about twenty years.

Ezekiel's writings reminded God's people that their sins had brought God's judgment on them. Chapters 1–24 were written before the fall of Jerusalem and warned of God's impending judgment on the city and the temple. In addition, Ezekiel had three key prophecies related to the end times—the preservation of a remnant of Israel, the overthrow of Gog, and a restored temple and sacrificial system during the reign of the Lord.

Ezekiel offered a word of encouragement to the citizens of Jerusalem in his prophecies. Despite their disobedience and deserving judgment, God would remain faithful to his covenant with Israel and ultimately defeat Judah's enemies (Ezekiel 25–32). "It is not for your sake, people of Israel, that I am going to do these things, but for the sake of my holy name" (Ezekiel 36:22). God also promised to gather his people and restore a remnant to their land.

I will bring them out from the nations and gather them from the countries, and I will bring them into their own land. I will pasture them on the mountains of Israel, in the ravines and in all the settlements in the land. (Ezekiel 34:13)

The first time this prophecy was fulfilled was during Judah's return to Jerusalem from captivity in Babylon and the rebuilding of the temple during the Medo-Persian reign. However, this prophecy possibly has a dual meaning in that not only was it fulfilled in the near future (or rather close to the time it was given), but it would also be fulfilled again in the end times. Israel did not remain in peace, but was dispersed again as it fell under attack by its enemies. This served as a warning that if the Jews did not learn their lesson and continued to sin, judgment would come again. It also served to encourage the Jews to repent, be patient, and trust in God's promise to deliver them once and for all from their trials.

Many believe that this prophecy was fulfilled again in 1948 with the reestablishment of the Jewish nation following the dispersion of the Jews. It is interesting to note, "Israel is the only nation that has ever been deported from her homeland, remained a distinct people while outside the land, and then returned to her original country."[28]

Other aspects of the prophecy related to the restoration of Israel were that Israel would hear the word of the Lord and that there would be "breath in you" (Ezekiel 37:6) implying spiritual renewal.

> [4] Then he said to me, "Prophesy to these bones and say to them, 'Dry bones, hear the word of the LORD! [5] This is what the Sovereign LORD says to these bones: I will make breath enter you, and you will come to life. [6] I will attach tendons to you and make flesh come upon you and cover you with skin; I will put breath in you, and you will come to life. Then you will know that I am the LORD." (Ezekiel 37:4–6)

Next, Ezekiel prophesied that Israel and Judah would become "one nation" (Ezekiel 37:22) and David would be "king over them" (Ezekiel

37:24) forever. This prophecy could be interpreted literally to refer to David reincarnated or as the Messiah, who was prophesied to be a descendant of David.

> [21] This is what the Sovereign LORD says: I will take the Israelites out of the nations where they have gone. I will gather them from all around and bring them back into their own land. [22] I will make them one nation in the land, on the mountains of Israel. There will be one king over all of them and they will never again be two nations or be divided into two kingdoms. [23] They will no longer defile themselves with their idols and vile images or with any of their offenses, for I will save them from all their sinful backsliding, and I will cleanse them. They will be my people, and I will be their God. [24] My servant David will be king over them, and they will all have one shepherd. They will follow my laws and be careful to keep my decrees. [25] … They and their children and their children's children will live there forever, and David my servant will be their prince forever. [26] I will make a covenant of peace with them; it will be an everlasting covenant. I will establish them and increase their numbers, and I will put my sanctuary among them forever. [27] My dwelling place will be with them; I will be their God, and they will be my people. [28] Then the nations will know that I the LORD make Israel holy, when my sanctuary is among them forever. (Ezekiel 37:21–28)

Ezekiel also prophesied the defeat of Israel's enemies and the overthrow of Gog. While some interpret this end-time battle to occur before the millennium, others interpret it as occurring after the millennium when Satan is released for a final time. Regardless of timing, from Ezekiel, we know that the invasion will come from the north and that the nations will be allied together against Israel.

The invasion will be initiated by "Gog, of the land of Magog, the chief prince of Meshek and Tubal" (Ezekiel 38:1). During the times of Ezekiel, Gog referred to the land north of the Black Sea. Today, parts of modern Russia and Turkey occupy this territory. Magog was the ancient land of the Scythians, which today includes parts of Central Asia and possibly Afghanistan. Meshech and Tubal are in modern Turkey. While the name of the country that will ultimately initiate this war is unclear, we can be sure they are enemies of God and this attack will come from the areas around the Black and Mediterranean seas. "Persia, Cush and Put will be with them, all with shields and helmets, also Gomer with all its troops, and Beth Togarmah from the far north with all its troops—its troops, and Beth Togarmah from the far north with all its troops— the many nations with you" (Ezekiel 38:4–5). "Persia is located to Israel's east, and Cush (Ethiopia) and Put (Libya) to the south; Gomer is the Cimmerians, a nomadic people north of the Black Sea, and Beth-Togarmah was on the border of Tubal. The confederation thus represents a world-wide alliance against Israel."[29]

The invasion will be on "a peaceful and unsuspecting people" (Ezekiel 38:11) with the intent to "plunder and loot" (Ezekiel 38:12) Israel. God will defend Israel. There will be "a great earthquake" (Ezekiel 38:19) in Israel so even "mountains will be overturned" (Ezekiel 38:20). The enemy will fight among themselves and ultimately be destroyed supernaturally by "rain, hailstones and burning sulfur" (Ezekiel 38:22). The result—"Nations will know that I the LORD am the Holy One in Israel" (Ezekiel 39:7).

Finally, Ezekiel foresaw the eventual victory and glorious reign of the Lord. Ezekiel 40–42 describes the dimensions of a temple that "the glory of the Lord" (Ezekiel 43:4–5) will fill. A sacrificial altar is built and the priesthood restored. The boundaries of the restored Promised Land are given, and it is divided among the twelve tribes. "And the name of the city from that time on will be: 'The Lord is there'" (Ezekiel 48:35).

Zechariah—Restoration of Israel

The book of Zechariah was written between 520 and 518 BC. During the reign of Cyrus, more than fifty thousand Jews returned to Palestine from Babylon in 538 BC and began to rebuild the temple. Zechariah's grandfather, Iddo, was a priest who returned from Babylon with Zerubbabel and Joshua. Zechariah encouraged the people to finish the temple and called for a spiritual change and repentance. He also prophesied about the Messiah's return. In regard to the end times, Zechariah prophesied there would be judgment for sin, a remnant of Israel would be saved, and the Messiah would return and rule in Jerusalem.

Zechariah depicted God's people as falling away, being punished, and being restored. There are numerous prophecies of the Messiah in these chapters, some of which refer to his first coming and others to his return a second time. In chapters 1 through 6, Zechariah had eight visions pertaining to the end times. In all these visions, the common theme was God's deliverance of his people and ultimate victory. In Zechariah 8:3, the Lord promised, "I will return to Zion and dwell in Jerusalem. Then Jerusalem will be called the Faithful City, and the mountain of the Lord Almighty will be called the Holy Mountain."

There are also numerous references to "that day," which is understood to refer to the day of the Lord and the end times. In Zechariah 9:16, he wrote, "The Lord their God will save his people on that day as a shepherd saves his flock." God promised that despite Israel's sin and the people being scattered to distant lands, "They will remember me. They and their children will survive, and they will return" (Zechariah 10:9) and repent. "They will look on me, the one they have pierced, and they will mourn for him as one mourns for an only child, and grieve bitterly for him as one grieves for a firstborn son" (Zechariah 12:10). Later in Zechariah 13, he stated that the one third remaining will be "put into the fire," refined "like silver" and tested "like gold" (Zechariah 13:9).

> [8] "In the whole land," declares the LORD, "two-thirds
> will be struck down and perish; yet one-third will be

left in it. ⁹ This third I will put into the fire; I will refine
them like silver and test them like gold. They will call
on my name and I will answer them; I will say, 'They
are my people,' and they will say, 'The LORD is our
God.'" (Zechariah 13:8–9)

In chapter 14, the Lord returned with his holy ones to Jerusalem
landing on the Mount of Olives and causing it to split.

On that day his feet will stand on the Mount of Olives,
east of Jerusalem, and the Mount of Olives will be split
in two from east to west, forming a great valley, with
half of the mountain moving north and half moving
south. (Zechariah 14:4)

Those who oppose the Lord will be destroyed. Worldwide worship
of the one true God will be established with nations coming annually to
Jerusalem during the Feast of the Tabernacles. "The Lord will be king
over the whole earth. On that day there will be one Lord, and his name
the only name" (Zechariah 14:9).

Malachi—Elijah Returns

The book of Malachi was written between 450 and 400 BC. it was
the last recorded prophecy of end times in the Old Testament. Malachi
means "my messenger." It is unclear who Malachi actually was; this
title could have referred simply to an anonymous writer. The book
was written following a period of revival under Nehemiah. The initial
enthusiasm of rebuilding the second temple and returning to Jerusalem
was starting to wear off. The people were going through the motions of
worship and tithing, but their hearts were growing cold. Malachi called
the people to repentance.

The main prophecy found in Malachi related to end times is of

Elijah's reappearance in Malachi 4 in the "great and dreadful day of the Lord" (Malachi 4:5).

> [1] "Surely the day is coming; it will burn like a furnace. All the arrogant and every evildoer will be stubble, and the day that is coming will set them on fire," says the LORD Almighty. "Not a root or a branch will be left to them. [2] But for you who revere my name, the sun of righteousness will rise with healing in its rays. And you will go out and frolic like well-fed calves. [3] Then you will trample on the wicked; they will be ashes under the soles of your feet on the day when I act," says the LORD Almighty. [4] "Remember the law of my servant Moses, the decrees and laws I gave him at Horeb for all Israel. [5] See, I will send the prophet Elijah to you before that great and dreadful day of the LORD comes. [6] He will turn the hearts of the parents to their children, and the hearts of the children to their parents; or else I will come and strike the land with total destruction." (Malachi 4:1–6)

Two references in the New Testament may point to how this prophecy will be fulfilled. The first reference is in Matthew 17. Jesus stated Elijah had already come in the person of John the Baptist.

> The disciples asked him, "Why then do the teachers of the law say that Elijah must come first?" Jesus replied, "To be sure, Elijah comes and will restore all things. But I tell you, Elijah has already come, and they did not recognize him, but have done to him everything they wished. In the same way the Son of Man is going to suffer at their hands." Then the disciples understood that he was talking to them about John the Baptist. (Matthew 17:10–13).

The second reference is in Revelation 11. Some believe Elijah will be one of the two witnesses who will come during the reign of the Antichrist: "And I will appoint my two witnesses, and they will prophesy for 1,260 days, clothed in sackcloth" (Revelation 11:3). This is based on three statements—that "fire comes from their mouths and devours their enemies" (Revelation 11:5), if anyone tries to harm them, they have "power to shut up the heavens so that it will not rain" (Revelation 11:6), and they are miraculously taken up to "heaven in a cloud" (Revelation 11:12). Elijah had these same powers as recorded in 1 and 2 Kings. Elijah told Ahab, "There will be neither dew nor rain in the next few years except at my word" (1 Kings 17:1), twice called fire "down from heaven" to consume "the captain and his men" (2 Kings 1:10, 12), and was miraculously taken "up to heaven in a whirlwind" (2 Kings 2:11). These similarities lead many to assume one of the witnesses is Elijah. However, there are also arguments for these witnesses being Moses, Enoch, or even two individuals not yet known. So a conclusive interpretation cannot be made at this time.

Judgment, Renewal, and Victory

The Old Testament prophets were speaking primarily to the Israelites. Their prophecies served as a warning of the consequences of sinful disobedience to God and the judgment that would follow. While it would be difficult times for the Israelites, the prophets encouraged them to repent and prophesied that God would restore them. God would be faithful to his covenants with the fathers of their faith, and in the end, the Messiah would come, destroy their enemies, and establish his kingdom.

In regard to the end times preceding the return of the Messiah to rule earth, the Old Testament prophets predicted many wars, several kingdoms rising and falling, the appearance of the abomination that causes desolation, heavenly upheaval, and an outpouring of the Holy Spirit. They also predicted the judgment and restoration of Israel, the return of a remnant to Israel, Messiah's return in the clouds in glory and power, and the establishment of his eternal kingdom. Many of these prophecies were echoed by Jesus as he prepared his disciples for the final days preceding his return

> God's response to rebellion is the destruction of sin, leading to repentance and purification of God's people and his creation.

Many prophets talked to God's people over several centuries. Just from those mentioned in this chapter starting with Joel in 835 BC through Malachi in 400 BC, time and again, God warned his people to obey him and not depart from his ways. Only in this way could they find the peace and prosperity God planned for them. But like today, humanity was stubborn and tried to find fulfillment apart from God.

God's response to rebellion is the destruction of sin, leading to repentance and purification of God's people and his creation. This cycle of sin, repentance, and restoration will continue in the end times with increasing intensity until sin is purged from this earth once and for all. Listen to God! Obey! And know the fullness of God's love and peace that can be found only through Him.

Bible Study Questions

Here is a list of Old Testament prophets who foresaw events in the end times. What did they see regarding the end times?

1. **Joel:** _____; outpouring
   of _____; heavenly _____;
   _____ battle.

2. **Isaiah:**_____for sin;_____
   of Israel; defeat of _____ and _____; the

_____ kingdom; and _____ heavens and earth.

3. **Micah:** Return of a remnant; future _____ of Israel.

4. **Zephaniah:** _____ for sin; _____ nations will be destroyed; survival of _____ in Israel.

5. **Ezekiel:** Judgment for sin; preservation of a _____ of Israel; overthrow of Judah's enemies, including _____; restored _____, sacrificial system and reign of the Lord.

6. **Zechariah:** Judgment for sin; a _____ of Israel would be saved; Messiah would return and rule in _____.

7. **Malachi:** _____ reappearance in the day of the Lord.

Reflection

God has been speaking to humanity and his people since the beginning of time. Prophecy after prophecy warned humanity about the consequences of sin. Is there an area of sin in your life God is speaking to you about?

PART 2

NEW TESTAMENT TEACHINGS ON END TIMES

CHAPTER 5

JESUS'S TEACHINGS ON THE SIGNS PRECEDING THE END TIMES

Be always on the watch, and pray that you may be
able to escape all that is about to happen, and that you
may be able to stand before the Son of Man.
—Luke 21:36

When you throw a rock into the water, waves ripple out from the center and expand. To get as close to the point of impact as possible to have the densest, tightest, and clearest vision, it seemed logical to look to the point where the ripples started; in this case, it is the teachings of Jesus. After all, who would know more about the end times than God himself? And amazingly, Jesus, the son of God, dwelt among us for a short time.

As the ripples begin to expand, the years move us further from the time when Jesus lived. In the first and second century, we see the writings of the apostles and early church providing eyewitness testimony and recent memory to the teachings of Jesus.

Jesus spoke with his disciples about the future and events that would occur up until the time he returned. He counseled his followers on how they should respond and live through these times. The primary teachings on this topic are found in Matthew 24–25, Luke 21, and Mark 13 and are referred to as the Olivet Discourse.

Before we go into that scripture, let's review the events from the days preceding. These events leading up to Jesus's teachings on Mount Olivet are important. They show the increased tension mounting between the religious leaders and Jesus. This tension would continue after Jesus's death and resurrection as the early church began to take root.

Days Preceding the Olivet Discourse

Jesus arrived in Bethany, near the Mount of Olives just outside Jerusalem. He sent his followers ahead to secure a donkey's colt and rode into Jerusalem on its back as the crowds shouted "Hosanna to the son of David! . . . Hosanna in the highest heaven!" (Matthew 21:9).

Imagine the angst of the religious leaders to see Jesus heralded in that way. "Hosanna" comes from a Hebrew word *howosiah-na* meaning "save now" or "save us, we pray." The crowd's use of this word at the triumphal entry was significant especially as they waved palm branches; by doing that, they were acknowledging Jesus as their Messiah. Their hope was that Jesus was the fulfillment of the Davidic covenant and that he had come to establish God's kingdom. Sadly, they didn't understand that salvation would come first and God's kingdom would come later.

Jesus went to the temple and overturned the tables of the money changers. He was outraged that the people were in one sense looking for a Messiah and yet in another displaying such a lack of respect for God's holiness in his temple. In Matthew 21:13, Jesus shouted, "My house shall be called a house of prayer and you have made it a den of robbers." The people's failure to understand God's Word, purpose, and plan were on full display.

The next day, Jesus was teaching once again in the temple. The chief priests challenged his authority, but they could not get him to say anything inappropriate. Finally, while he was teaching to the crowds, the Pharisees and Sadducees set out to trick him. Jesus turned the tables and instead of falling for their schemes, he called out their true character and labeled them hypocrites and vipers.

These events were leading up to Jesus's crucifixion. The religious leaders were furious about his teachings and looked for a way to arrest him. Rather than be convicted of their sinful actions and deceit, they sought to kill the man who was righteous and without sin.

As Jesus sat with his disciples on Mount Olivet toward the end of the week, he knew his time on earth was drawing to a close. The Olivet Discourse covered two key prophecies by Jesus—the destruction of the temple and the remaining days until Jesus returned.

Destruction of the Temple

As Jesus and his disciples walked by the temple, they marveled at the feat of architecture and magnificence of the structure. Jesus told them it would be destroyed completely; not one stone would be left. At that point, they asked a few questions. The first question was about the destruction of the temple: "When will this be?" Luke 21:20–24 records Jesus's answer.

> [20] When you see Jerusalem being surrounded by armies, you will know that its desolation is near. [21] Then let those who are in Judea flee to the mountains, let those in the city get out, and let those in the country not enter the city. [22] For this is the time of punishment in fulfillment of all that has been written. [23] How dreadful it will be in those days for pregnant women and nursing mothers! There will be great distress in the land and wrath against this people. [24] They will fall by the sword and will be taken as prisoners to all the nations. Jerusalem will be trampled on by the Gentiles until the times of the Gentiles are fulfilled. (Luke 21:20–24)

Jesus prophesied, "When you see Jerusalem being surrounded by armies, you will know that its desolation is near." Historically, the destruction of the temple followed several decades later in AD 70, when the Roman legions of Titus besieged and captured Jerusalem.

Jesus's words served as a down payment for the rest of his response and prophetic warnings. The disciples had asked about the destruction of the temple and the end times. Jesus answered both questions though the two events would not take place at the same time. This is referred to as dual reference and is a common technique of prophets.

Dual reference is the use and fulfillment of a more-immediate event to foreshadow a future event. Quite often in scripture, a prophecy will have both short- and long-term significance. The short-term prophecy will take place in a few years so the accuracy of the prophet can be validated; it will serve as a guarantee of the future prophecy. The long-term prophecy often does not occur in the lifetime of the prophet.

Signs of Jesus's Return

The second question asked by the disciples was, "What will be the sign of your coming and the end of the age?" At first glance, this seems like an odd question to follow their question about the temple's destruction. Possibly, the disciples thought the temple destruction and Jesus's kingdom would occur at the same time.

Jesus's answer is in Matthew 24:3–35. Parallel scriptures in Luke 21 and Mark 13 also record this response. Consider for a moment what the disciples might have been thinking about this teacher, Jesus. What might have been their perspective at that point? What had they witnessed since their calling to follow Jesus by the Sea of Galilee?

They had seen many miracles of Jesus—the feeding of the 5,000, the healing of the sick, and the raising of Lazarus to name a few. They had witnessed him walking on water in the Sea of Galilee. They had heard his passionate and accurate teaching in the temple. They seemed to be finally grasping that Jesus was more than a prophet—that he was the Messiah. Yet was it possible they were looking for a Messiah to bring both salvation and political leadership? Were they expecting Jesus to set up his kingdom in the near future and overturn the Romans? Did they understand there would be another coming, a separate event, in fulfillment of the prophecies? Whatever their thought process, Jesus responded with what they needed to know about the signs that would precede his return.

Jesus identified several signs that would precede his coming and the end of the age. They were false messiahs, wars, famines, pestilence and earthquakes, unrest among nations, the persecution of the saints, the spread of the gospel, the abomination that causes desolation standing in the holy place, the false messiah performing signs, and heavenly upheaval. (See exhibit 2.)

False Messiahs

The first sign we are warned about is false messiahs (Matthew 24:4–6; Mark 13:5). In Mark 13:6, we read, "Many will come in my name, claiming, 'I am he,' and will deceive many."

This sign is prophesied along with a warning for believers: "Watch out that no one deceives you" (Matthew 24:4). Luke added, "Do not follow them" (Luke 21:8). How could such individuals deceive true believers? First, they will claim to be the Messiah. Second, Luke 21:8 adds they will claim, "The time is near." So essentially, these heretics are claiming to be the impersonation of the Messiah as he returns to reign.

Surely, people would grow wise to their schemes once the other prophesies related to the Messiah's kingdom had not materialized. Yet Jesus told his followers that these false messiahs would deceive some in the church.

Wars, Famines, Pestilence, Earthquakes, and Unrest among Nations

The second set of signs Jesus prophesied included wars, unrest among nations, famines, pestilence, earthquakes, and heavenly signs (Matthew 24:6–8; Luke 21:9–11; Mark 13:7). These signs were not limited in impact to believers; all humanity would be affected. Many events were listed in these few short verses. Let's take them bit by bit.

> [9] "When you hear of wars and uprisings, do not be frightened. These things must happen first, but the end will not come right away." [10] Then he said to them: "Nation will rise against nation, and kingdom against kingdom. [11] There will be great earthquakes, famines and pestilences in various places, and fearful events and great signs from heaven." (Luke 21:9–11)

First, Jesus spoke of wars, rumors of wars, and unrest between nations. The wars since the beginning of history are too numerous to count. They will continue and increase in intensity until the Son of Man returns. Humanity's ability to find peace will evaporate and hostilities will increase. Even when relationships between nations don't deteriorate to physical battle or wars, alliances will break down and relationships will totter on the brink of war.

Second, Jesus foresaw that humanity's ability to feed itself would be compromised. Famines caused by droughts, infertile lands, and lands ravaged by war and insects would be rampant across the globe. Luke 21:11 adds pestilences—diseases such as the bubonic plague that can kill thousands to the list of natural and human disasters. We already see this in many parts of the world.

In Revelation, in the midst of the many judgments that will fall on humanity, ultimately a fourth of the world will die as a result of these tragedies.

> I looked, and there before me was a pale horse! Its rider was named Death, and Hades was following close behind him. They were given power over a fourth of the earth to kill by sword, famine and plague, and by the wild beasts of the earth. (Revelation 6:8)

And finally, even the stability and surety in the ground beneath our feet and heavens above will be shaken through earthquakes and heavenly signs. The familiar storms, earthquakes, and other natural disasters are a part of our everyday experience. But scientists frequently warn us of more events that could occur such as an epic meteor strike with the potential to wipe out thousands and throw us into a worldwide winter, or solar flares, or a powerful volcanic explosion capable of wiping out large parts of a continent.

We see all of these happenings today to some degree in various places around the world. Matthew stated, "All these are the beginning of birth pains" (Matthew 24:8). As the time of Jesus's return gets nearer, the scriptures above indicate the degree and intensity of these events will increase just as the pains of childbirth intensify in a woman's labor as the time for birth gets closer.

Persecution of Saints and the Spread of the Gospel

Jesus warned his followers there would be persecution of the saints (Matthew 24:9–13; Luke 21:12–19; Mark 13:9–13). This persecution will occur before the tribulation to some degree and even in greater intensity during the tribulation. In the context of persecution, Jesus warned us again of false prophets. In Luke and Mark, we learn that this persecution may even come from our immediate families.

> [9] Then you will be handed over to be persecuted and put to death, and you will be hated by all nations because of me. [10] At that time many will turn away from the faith and will betray and hate each other, [11] and many false prophets will appear and deceive many people. [12] Because of the increase of wickedness, the love of most will grow cold, [13] but the one who stands firm to the end will be saved. (Matthew 24:9–13)

Jesus talked about persecution of the saints in several other places in the Gospels. In John 15:18–25 and John 16:1–4, Jesus taught that his followers would be persecuted just as he was persecuted. Inasmuch as Christians are a reflection of their master, it stands to reason that the world will respond to their message in the same way it responded to the message of Jesus. Jesus reminded his followers, "If the world hates you, keep in mind that it hated me first" (John 15:18). The root of this hatred and persecution is a deep-seated hatred of the Father (John 15:23), distortion of the truth (John 15:25, 16:2), and hearts that do not truly know God (John 16:3).

In Matthew 24:14, another sign of the end of the age was prophesied—the preaching of the gospel to the whole world. This is a testament to the unwavering character of those who love the Lord and continue to share the hope of their salvation in the midst of persecution. It is also a beautiful example of faith and obedience. In Mark 16:15, Jesus commanded his followers to "Go into all the world and preach the gospel to all creation."

This outpouring of faith and obedience flows in response to a loving and forgiving God and is linked to an outcome: "Then the end will come" (Matthew 24:14). Believers in partnership with God and empowered by the Holy Spirit preach the gospel thus planting the seed and hope of salvation, which is brought to fruition by God.

Abomination that Causes Desolation in the Holy Place

As we continue in the list of end-time signs that will culminate in Jesus's return, we can almost hear the hoofbeats quickening as the time of his return gets closer. What began as lies and deceit progresses to famine, disease, and unrest between nations and deteriorates further into the persecution of believers and open opposition to God. Now, we come to the embodiment of Satan in the form of a world leader standing in the holy place in Jerusalem (Matthew 24:15–22; Luke 21:20–24; Mark 13:14–19). The "abomination that causes desolation" is an excerpt from Daniel's prophecy: "And at the temple he will set up an abomination that causes desolation, until the end that is decreed is poured out on him" (Daniel 9:27).

> [15] So when you see standing in the holy place "the abomination that causes desolation," spoken of through

the prophet Daniel—let the reader understand—
[16] then let those who are in Judea flee to the mountains.
(Matthew 24:15–16)

[22] For this is the time of punishment in fulfillment of all
that has been written. [23] How dreadful it will be in those
days for pregnant women and nursing mothers! There
will be great distress in the land and wrath against
this people. [24] They will fall by the sword and will be
taken as prisoners to all the nations. Jerusalem will
be trampled on by the Gentiles until the times of the
Gentiles are fulfilled. (Luke 21:22–24)

This will be a dreadful time particularly for those in Judea. The
direction Jesus gave in previous signs— "don't be deceived" by false
messiahs, "don't be alarmed" by wars and famines, and "stand firm"
during persecution—seem calm in contrast to the strong and urgent
warning he gives at this point—flee! You can sense the danger. Jesus
soberly tells his followers that these will be days of distress unequaled
from the beginning of time. From the book of Daniel, we know that
once we see this event, it will be only a few short years before the
Messiah's return.

From other scriptures, we know that the individual who is this
"abomination" hates the people of God. We learn that this man will be
unlawful and disrespect the religious and holy practices of the temple.
But he will not stop with disrespecting the teachings of God; the
scriptures warn that many will "fall by the sword and will be taken as
prisoners" (Luke 21:24).

The desolation in the temple caused by this individual takes many
forms. In 167 BC, a Greek ruler by the name of Antiochus Epiphanes
set up an altar to Zeus in the Jewish temple in Jerusalem and sacrificed a
pig on the altar. Antiochus typified the Antichrist. Thus, we expect the
desolation to be similar—to include the sacrifice of unholy animals and
the improper worship of a false god. Also, in Revelation 13:12, people
will be made to "worship the first beast," which is sometimes referred to

as the Antichrist. This will be a dark time for God's people, but by the grace of God, it will be limited to forty-two months (Revelation 13:5).

False Messiahs, Prophets, and Signs

After the abomination that causes desolation stands in the holy place, the remaining signs increase to an apex of intensity. Once again, Jesus warned us of false messiahs, but added false prophets, signs, and wonders (Matthew 24:23–26; Luke 21:20–23). Deceit and lies punctuated by demonic powers will be rampant. In Mark 13:20, Jesus told us the times would be so intense that if "the Lord had not cut short those days, no one would survive."

> [23] At that time if anyone says to you, "Look, here is the Messiah!" or, "There he is!" do not believe it. [24] For false messiahs and false prophets will appear and perform great signs and wonders to deceive, if possible, even the elect. [25] See, I have told you ahead of time. [26] So if anyone tells you, "There he is, out in the wilderness," do not go out; or, "Here he is, in the inner rooms," do not believe it. [27] For as lightning that comes from the east is visible even in the west, so will be the coming of the Son of Man. (Matthew 24: 23–27)

Jesus told us not to believe the lies and ungodly works of these false messiahs and to be on our guard. Why do you think he added we should be "on guard" to his previous warning of "don't be deceived," the direction given with the first time he mentioned false messiahs? This time in history will follow the abomination standing in the holy place in Jerusalem. Satan knows his time of ruling this earth is coming to an end. Like a caged cat, he will be lashing out at God's chosen people. Undoubtedly, these will be dangerous times. Christians and Jews will be looking for their Messiah to rescue them and may become vulnerable and frightened. This fear can result in them becoming victims of the great deceiver, Satan. There will be few who can be trusted during these times. Christians must be well grounded and stand firm in the truth of the holy scriptures. They must study and know the truth so that they will be able to recognize lies.

Heavenly Upheaval

The last sign Jesus says will occur before the end of the age and his return is heavenly upheaval (Matthew 24:29; Luke 21:25–26; Mark 13:24–25). These include the sun being darkened, the moon not giving light, stars falling from the sky, and heavenly bodies shaken.

> [25] There will be signs in the sun, moon and stars. On the earth, nations will be in anguish and perplexity at the roaring and tossing of the sea. [26] People will faint from terror, apprehensive of what is coming on the world, for the heavenly bodies will be shaken. (Luke 21:25–26)

Jesus also briefly alluded to the effect and distress of the end times as he was being led away by the soldiers to be crucified. In Luke 23:29–30, he said, "For the time will come when you will say, 'Blessed are the childless women, the wombs that never bore and the breasts that never nursed!' Then they will say to the mountains, 'Fall on us!' and to the hills, 'Cover us!'"

Make no mistake—the heavenly upheaval prophesied here is not even close to what we see today with meteors flashing across the sky or solar and lunar eclipses. The Bible says people will "faint with terror." These events will be catastrophic beyond our current experience and imagination.

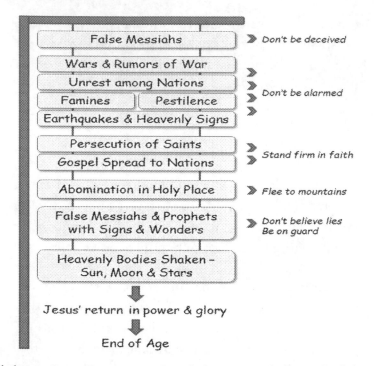

Exhibit 2. Signs Pointing to Jesus's Return and the End of the Age

A Need to Know

Why did Jesus tell his disciples these prophecies? Perhaps there were several reasons. First, Jesus told his disciples what would happen so they would "not fall away" when times became difficult (John 16:1). Second, he told them so when they saw the signs occurring, they would "know that [Jesus's return] is near, right at the door" (Mark 13:29).

Knowing that Jesus will return and be victorious over Satan gives Christians hope. But it also reminds us that we are to be witnesses and make disciples with increased urgency so no Christian will be left behind. And finally, perhaps he told them about the things that were coming so they would not be caught unprepared but instead "be able to stand before the Son of Man" (Luke 21:36).

Bible Study Questions

1. **Dual reference** is the use and fulfillment of a more _____ event to foreshadow a _____ event to come.

Signs given by Jesus

2. False _____ (Matthew 24:4–5, Luke 21:8; Mark 13:5)

3. _____, unrest among nations, _____, pestilence, _____, and heavenly signs (Matthew 24:6–8, Luke 21:9–11, Mark 13:7).

4. Persecution of _____ and gospel spread to nations (Matthew 24:9–14, Luke 21:12–19, Mark 13:9–13).

5. _____ in holy place (Matthew 24:15–22, Luke 21:20–24, Mark 13:14–19).

6. False messiahs and prophets with _____ and _____ (Matthew 24:23–26, Luke 21:20–23).

7. Heavenly _____ (Matthew 24:29; Luke 21:25–26; Mark 13:24–25).

Reflection

Why do you think Jesus wanted us to be aware of the signs preceding his return to establish his kingdom?

CHAPTER 6

JESUS'S RETURN: AN EVENT NO ONE WILL OVERLOOK

For as lightning that comes from the east is visible even in
the west, so will be the coming of the Son of Man.
—Matthew 24:27

After the signs have been fulfilled, Jesus will return. The scriptures describe this event as sudden and unexpected and accompanied by powerful heavenly signs seen by all.

First, Jesus's return will be sudden and unexpected. In Paul's letter to the Thessalonians, he wrote,

> [1] Now, brothers and sisters, about times and dates we do not need to write to you, [2] for you know very well that the day of the Lord will come like a thief in the night. [3] While people are saying, "Peace and safety," destruction will come on them suddenly, as labor pains on a pregnant woman, and they will not escape. (1 Thessalonians 5:1–3)

Labor pains do not begin until shortly before delivery time, and they increase in frequency until the baby is born. In the same way, the preceding signs connected with the Lord's return will begin shortly before his return and increase in frequency and intensity building up to the culmination, the Messiah's return.

Second, Jesus's return will be accompanied by heavenly signs. Jesus said his return would be like lightning in that it would be sudden and visible in the sky (Matthew 24:27). Then, the sign of the Son of Man will appear in heaven (Matthew 24:30). The Bible does not specify what this sign will be, but it does say everyone will recognize and see it.

> [27] For as lightning that comes from the east is visible even in the west, so will be the coming of the Son of Man … [30] Then will appear the sign of the Son of Man in heaven. And then all the peoples of the earth will mourn when they see the Son of Man coming on the clouds of heaven, with power and great glory. (Matthew 24: 27, 30)

The reaction to this sign and event is that "peoples of the earth will mourn" (Matthew 24:30). You would almost expect rejoicing and excitement at such an amazing and incredible day when the Lord returns, yet the people mourn. Could it be they will be convicted of their sin and aware of impending judgment? Do they know they are facing sure defeat? Perhaps they will realize the abomination and the false prophet have misled them. Those who believe will be swept up into heaven to join their Lord. But for others, judgment awaits.

Third, Jesus's return will be powerful and seen by all. Jesus said the Son of Man would come in the clouds with great power and glory (Matthew 24:30, 26:64; Mark 13:26; Luke 21:27–28).

> [27] At that time they will see the Son of Man coming in a cloud with power and great glory. [28] When these things begin to take place, stand up and lift up your heads, because your redemption is drawing near. (Luke 21:27–28)

After Jesus was resurrected from the dead and had visited with his disciples, he was taken up to heaven. Two men dressed in white, presumably angels, suddenly appeared and told the disciples watching his ascension, "'Men of Galilee,' they said, 'why do you stand here looking into the sky? This same Jesus, who has been taken from you into heaven, will come back in the same way you have seen him go into heaven'" (Acts 1:11).

Finally, Jesus said that when he returned, his angels would gather his elect (Mark 13:27) and "And he will send his angels with a loud trumpet call, and they will gather his elect from the four winds, from one end of the heavens to the other" (Matthew 24:31).

Parables about Jesus's Return

Immediately following Jesus's response to his disciples regarding the signs of the end of the age, he told a series of parables that further explained what his return would be like. Often, these parables are studied as stand-alone messages. However, it is best to study them in the context in which they were given—that is, as an illustration of the time when Jesus returns.

A parable uses something familiar to help us understand something heavenly or spiritual. In each of the parables, Jesus warned us that his return would be unexpected. This calls for the Christian to be in a perpetual state of readiness and diligence in obeying God.

While all share the common theme of the suddenness of his return, each parable has a slightly different emphasis. They include the parable of the fig tree, the parable of the days of Noah and Lot, the parables of the thief and obedient servants, and the parable of the ten virgins.

Parable of the Fig Tree

The first parable given is one of a fig tree (Matthew 24:32–35; Luke 21:29–33; Mark 13:28–31). Fig trees were commonplace in Israel and around Jerusalem. When Jesus spoke about the season for a fig tree to sprout leaves and bear fruit, the answer was well known.

> [29] He told them this parable: "Look at the fig tree and all the trees. [30] When they sprout leaves, you can see for yourselves and know that summer is near. [31] Even so, when you see these things happening, you know that the kingdom of God is near. [32] Truly I tell you, this generation will certainly not pass away until all these things have happened. [33] Heaven and earth will pass away, but my words will never pass away." (Luke 21:29–33)

The main message of this parable is that once you see the signs, you will know the time is near. With a fig tree, you know that the time is getting near for it to bear fruit when the twigs get tender and its leaves come out. Jesus taught that a "generation" would not pass away from the time these signs begin.

The meaning of a generation has been interpreted in different ways. Some say this means that the time from when the signs begin until the return of Jesus will be a human lifespan. However, the Greek word *genea* can also refer to the time between two key events, an era, or the span of a nation. Since it has been close to 2,000 years since Jesus ascended into heaven, it is safe to assume that in this context, generation refers to a period between two key events.

Though we are not given a specific time of Jesus's return, the certainty of the end of this timespan is emphasized by Jesus. "Heaven and earth will pass away, but my words will never pass away" (Luke 21:33). We can be sure that as we see these signs transpire, Jesus's return is not far away.

Parable of the Days of Noah and Lot

In Matthew 24:36–41 and Luke 17:26–32, Jesus further compared the suddenness of his return to the days of Noah and Lot, a time when people were preoccupied with daily affairs of business and self-indulgence, ignoring God's ways, engrossed in their sin, and unrepentant. Destruction overtook them suddenly, without warning, and none could escape.

> [26] Just as it was in the days of Noah, so also will it be in the days of the Son of Man. [27] People were eating, drinking, marrying and being given in marriage up to the day Noah entered the ark. Then the flood came and destroyed them all. [28] It was the same in the days of Lot. People were eating and drinking, buying and selling, planting and building. [29] But the day Lot left Sodom, fire and sulfur rained down from heaven and destroyed them all. [30] It will be just like this on the day the Son of Man is revealed. [31] On that day no one who is on the housetop, with possessions inside, should go down to get them. Likewise, no one in the field should go back for anything. [32] Remember Lot's wife! [33] Whoever tries to keep their life will lose it, and whoever loses their life will preserve it. (Luke 17:26–33)

The key message of this parable is to warn all believers and unbelievers alike that Jesus's return will be sudden and unexpected. The time to repent is now, not tomorrow or some undetermined date in the future.

Parables of the Thief and Obedient Servants

In the parables of the thief and the obedient servants (Matthew 24:42–44, 45–51; Mark 14:32–36), once again, we are told Jesus's return will be sudden and unexpected. Only this time, the message is for believers! Believers are exhorted to be ready, keep watch, and be faithful and wise.

In the parable of the thief, Jesus pointed out the obvious. If the owner knew when he was going to be robbed, he would have been ready. The only remedy for not knowing when an event will occur is to be in a constant state of readiness.

> [42] Therefore keep watch, because you do not know on what day your Lord will come. [43] But understand this: If the owner of the house had known at what time of night the thief was coming, he would have kept watch and would not have let his house be broken into. [44] So you also must be ready, because the Son of Man will come at an hour when you do not expect him. (Matthew 24:42–44)

Likewise, in the parable of the owner who had left his servants in charge, his return was at an unspecified time. Unfortunately, for some servants, he caught them slacking in their responsibilities. Once again, a continued state of readiness is the best remedy.

> [32] But about that day or hour no one knows, not even the angels in heaven, nor the Son, but only the Father. [33] Be on guard! Be alert! You do not know when that time will come. [34] It's like a man going away: He leaves his house and puts his servants in charge, each with their assigned task, and tells the one at the door to keep watch. [35] Therefore keep watch because you do not know when the owner of the house will come back— whether in the evening, or at midnight, or when the rooster crows, or at dawn. [36] If he comes suddenly, do not let him find you sleeping. [37] What I say to you, I say to everyone: "Watch!" (Mark 13:32–37)

As days pass and we don't see Jesus's return, it will be tempting to think there is plenty of time to get our lives on the right path or to do the right thing. Jesus is saying, "Don't dawdle! Get with the program today!" We shouldn't put off until tomorrow doing what God has called us to do today. Jesus's return could come any day. And when he returns, we want our Lord to find that we have been faithful and obedient servants and that we are prepared to follow him for eternity because we are already doing it.

Parable of the Ten Virgins

Next, Jesus compared his return to that of a wedding (Matthew 25:1–13) where the bridegroom's return has been delayed. The wedding party was waiting late into the night. In this parable, Jesus warned those who were close to Him to be ready. Once again, he told us to keep watch as his return would be unexpected.

> [1] At that time the kingdom of heaven will be like ten virgins who took their lamps and went out to meet the bridegroom. [2] Five of them were foolish and five were wise. [3] The foolish ones took their lamps but did not take any oil with them. [4] The wise ones, however, took oil in jars along with their lamps. [5] The bridegroom was a long time in coming, and they all became drowsy and fell asleep. [6] At midnight the cry rang out: "Here's the bridegroom! Come out to meet him!"
>
> [7] Then all the virgins woke up and trimmed their lamps. [8] The foolish ones said to the wise, "Give us some of your oil; our lamps are going out." [9] "No," they replied, "there may not be enough for both us and you. Instead, go to those who sell oil and buy some for yourselves." [10] But while they were on their way to buy the oil, the bridegroom arrived. The virgins who were ready went

in with him to the wedding banquet. And the door was shut. [11] Later the others also came. "Lord, Lord," they said, "open the door for us!" [12] But he replied, "Truly I tell you, I don't know you." [13] Therefore keep watch, because you do not know the day or the hour. (Matthew 25:1–12)

In other scriptures, the analogy of a bride and wedding are used to represent Jesus and the body of believers. Revelation 19:7 reads, "Let us rejoice and be glad and give him glory! For the wedding of the Lamb has come, and his bride has made herself ready."

As we look at this parable, we see two types of individuals—wise people who had enough oil and foolish people who did not. The wedding represents the Lord's return and those who will be invited to be in his kingdom. Those who are wise have heard the Word of the Lord and received his salvation. Those who are foolish have also heard the Word of the Lord but have put off repentance and receiving salvation. Those who have received the good news of Christ, repented of their sins, and follow Jesus in truth will be saved. However, some in the church are insincere and not truly following God similar to the Pharisees and Sadducees during Jesus's time. "Thus, by their fruit you will recognize them" (Matthew 7:20). When the Lord returns suddenly, it will be too late for them to change. Be ready, the Lord warns.

Other Scriptures in Which Jesus Talked about His Return and the End of the Age

We have observed a few messages to believers in the verses above on how Christians should live their lives as they see these signs preceding his return. In the remainder of Jesus's teachings in the Olivet Discourse in Matthew 25, Jesus continued to address how we should live as we wait for the Lord's return. He added that we should bear fruit and be compassionate to those in need.

Parable of Bags of Gold

Jesus told a parable of a master who entrusted three of his servants with portions of his wealth while he went on a journey (Matthew 25:14–30). To one of the servants, he gave five bags of gold, to another, he gave two bags of gold, and to the third, he gave one bag of gold. In this parable, the master is analogous to Jesus. The bags of gold represent the treasure he has given us in the good news of the gospel and spiritual gifts.

> [14] Again, it will be like a man going on a journey, who called his servants and entrusted his wealth to them. [15] To one he gave five bags of gold, to another two bags, and to another one bag, each according to his ability. Then he went on his journey. [16] The man who had received five bags of gold went at once and put his money to work and gained five bags more. [17] So also, the one with two bags of gold gained two more. [18] But the man who had received one bag went off, dug a hole in the ground and hid his master's money. [19] After a long time the master of those servants returned and settled accounts with them. [20] The man who had received five bags of gold brought the other five. "Master," he said, "you entrusted me with five bags of gold. See, I have gained five more." [21] His master replied, "Well done, good and faithful servant! You have been faithful with a few things; I will put you in charge of many things. Come and share your master's happiness!"

> [22] The man with two bags of gold also came. "Master," he said, "you entrusted me with two bags of gold; see, I have gained two more." [23] His master replied, "Well done, good and faithful servant! You have been faithful with a few things; I will put you in charge of many things. Come and share your master's happiness!"

²⁴ Then the man who had received one bag of gold came. "Master," he said, "I knew that you are a hard man, harvesting where you have not sown and gathering where you have not scattered seed. ²⁵ So I was afraid and went out and hid your gold in the ground. See, here is what belongs to you." ²⁶ His master replied, "You wicked, lazy servant! So you knew that I harvest where I have not sown and gather where I have not scattered seed? ²⁷ Well then, you should have put my money on deposit with the bankers, so that when I returned I would have received it back with interest. ²⁸ So take the bag of gold from him and give it to the one who has ten bags. ²⁹ For whoever has will be given more, and they will have an abundance. Whoever does not have, even what they have will be taken from them. ³⁰ And throw that worthless servant outside, into the darkness, where there will be weeping and gnashing of teeth." (Matthew 25:14–30)

We see different responses of believers. Some will hide their treasure, and others will be fruitful. Not everyone receives the same level of spiritual gifts due to different levels of capability, but it is clear we should not hide or bury what we have received. Instead, we are to use those gifts to God's glory. Also, this parable teaches that there is greater accountability for believers with more gifts and talents.

> Jesus intended us to share the good news with others, to invest and use our spiritual gifts, and to live righteous and obedient lives.

In other parts of Matthew, Jesus taught a similar message using different analogies. Jesus believers are compared to "light" in darkness and "salt" to the earth (Matthew 5:13–16). Jesus intended us to share the good news with others, to invest and use our spiritual gifts, and to live righteous and obedient lives.

In summary, this parable teaches us to be good and faithful servants and that we will receive judgment based on our works.

Comparison of Sheep and Goats

As Jesus wrapped up his discourse with his disciples on the Mount of Olives, he gave one final example that warned of judgment based on our works. In this parable in Matthew, the shepherd is analogous to Jesus, the sheep are his followers, and the goats are unbelievers.

> [32] All the nations will be gathered before him, and he will separate the people one from another as a shepherd separates the sheep from the goats. [33] He will put the sheep on his right and the goats on his left. [34] Then the King will say to those on his right, "Come, you who are blessed by my Father; take your inheritance, the kingdom prepared for you since the creation of the world. [35] For I was hungry and you gave me something to eat, I was thirsty and you gave me something to drink, I was a stranger and you invited me in, [36] I needed clothes and you clothed me, I was sick and you looked after me, I was in prison and you came to visit me ..."

> [40] The King will reply, "Truly I tell you, whatever you did for one of the least of these brothers and sisters of mine, you did for me." [41] Then he will say to those on his left, "Depart from me, you who are cursed, into the eternal fire prepared for the devil and his angels. [42] For I was hungry and you gave me nothing to eat, I was thirsty and you gave me nothing to drink, [43] I was a stranger and you did not invite me in, I needed clothes and you did not clothe me, I was sick and in prison and

you did not look after me." …[45] He will reply, "Truly I tell you, whatever you did not do for one of the least of these, you did not do for me." (Matthew 25:32–36, 40–45)

The sheep had lived obedient lives, showing compassion for strangers, the poor, and the sick. The goats had been insensitive to the needs of those around them. The judgment of "eternal punishment" referred to here is reserved for unbelievers, but there will be a judgment of works for believers. Jesus warned that our actions were an important part of exercising our faith. Just as Jesus showed great compassion for us, we are to show compassion to others.

In all these parables, we are reminded that Jesus will return when we least expect it! It will be too late to fix any decisions or to rethink an action. Our only recourse is to be ready and living in a way that pleases God.

[34] Be careful, or your hearts will be weighed down with carousing, drunkenness and the anxieties of life, and that day will close on you suddenly like a trap. [35] For it will come on all those who live on the face of the whole earth. [36] Be always on the watch, and pray that you may be able to escape all that is about to happen, and that you may be able to stand before the Son of Man. (Luke 21:34–36)

Bible Study Questions

1. **Describing the return of Jesus …**
   - Sudden and unexpected
   - Like _____ (Matthew 24:27)
   - _____ in heaven (Matthew 24:30a)
   - People will _____ (Matthew 24:30b)

- Clouds, _____, _____ (Matthew 24:30b, Luke 21:27–28, Mark 13:26)
- Gathering of _____ (Matthew 24:31, Mark 13:27)

2. A **parable** uses something _____ to help us understand something _____ or spiritual.

3. **Parables about Jesus's Return**
   - Fig Tree (Matthew 24:32–35; Luke 21:29–33; Mark 13:28–31)—Once you see the signs, you will know the time is _____.
   - Days of Noah (Matthew 24:36–41—Coming will be sudden and _____.
   - Thief Breaking into House (Matthew 24:42–44)—Be _____; coming will be unexpected.
   - Obedient Servants (Matthew 24:45–51; Mark 13:32–36)—Return unexpected; be _____ and _____; keep watch; be ready.
   - Ten Virgins (Matthew 25:1–13)—Be ready; keep watch; return unexpected.

4. **Parables regarding Believer's Call to Action**
   - Bags of Gold (Matthew 25:14–30)—Be _____ and _____ servants; _____ for unfaithful.
   - Sheep and Goats (Matthew 25:31–46)—Compassion for _____, _____ and _____; judgment for goats.

Reflection

Are you ready for the Lord's return? If you knew Jesus was coming tomorrow, what would you change today?

CHAPTER 7

APOSTLES' TEACHINGS ON END TIMES

Therefore go and make disciples of all nations, baptizing them
in the name of the Father and of the Son and of the Holy Spirit,
and teaching them to obey everything I have commanded you.
And surely I am with you always, to the very end of the age.
—Matthew 28:19–20

Jesus's last words to his beloved disciples before ascending into heaven
are recorded in Acts 1:1-11. For the forty days following his resurrection,
Jesus met often with his apostles, "gave many convincing proofs that
he was alive" and "spoke about the kingdom of God" (Acts 1:3). It was
apparent that Jesus was considering the days that lay before his precious
followers. Knowing they would have to endure many hardships, he did
not leave them alone. He left the Holy Spirit (Acts 1:5) with them to
teach, guide, and empower them until he returned.

Jesus's Parting Words

After witnessing his resurrection, once again, his disciples asked
him, "Lord, are you at this time going to restore the kingdom to Israel?"
(Acts 1:6). The disciples still didn't fully understand what Jesus's return
would look like or even that there would be a delay before his return. Or
they might have reasoned that possibly his resurrection was the return

he had been talking about. But Jesus's response made it clear that the time had not yet come.

Before he ascended into heaven, Jesus left his believers with three key points.

- "It is not for you to know the times or dates the Father has set by his own authority" (Acts 1:7),
- You are not alone—the Holy Spirit will be with you and he will give you power in the days to come (Acts 1:8), and
- You will "be my witnesses in Jerusalem, and in all Judea and Samaria, and to the ends of the earth" (Acts 1:8).

First, they were reminded they would not know the time of Jesus's return. This message must have sounded similar to the parables he told them on Mount Olivet regarding the sudden, unexpected nature of his return. Undoubtedly, it is tempting to try to calculate the day and year of Jesus's return. Perhaps in knowing, we deceive ourselves into thinking we can somehow stop sinning just in the nick of time. Or perhaps we will be even more attentive to living righteously and demonstrating our godly works as the time draws nearer. But as we saw in this response and in Jesus's parables on the end times, Jesus was teaching his followers to be ready at all times living in a constant state of obedience and righteousness.

> Jesus was teaching his followers to be ready at all times living in a constant state of obedience and righteousness.

Next, Jesus comforted his followers by letting them know he was not leaving them alone in keeping his commands and dealing with opposition to their faith whether in the form of government, church, or spiritually. In John 14:16–17, Jesus said, "And I will ask the Father, and he will give you another advocate to help you and be with you forever— [17] the Spirit of truth." Later, before he ascended to heaven, he reminded them, "Do not leave Jerusalem, but wait for the gift my Father promised ... in a few days you will be baptized with the Holy Spirit" (Acts 1:4–5). Several times, Jesus emphasized the companionship of the Holy Spirit. This relationship is an integral part of a Christian's life today. The obedient and righteous lives we are exhorted to live are possible only with the power of the Holy Spirit living in us.

Third, Jesus stated the primary purpose and mission of believers in the end times: "You will be my witnesses" (Acts 1:8). As we consider the broken and sinful world we will have to endure and reside in until Jesus returns, we will be salt and light to an unsaved people (Matthew 5:13–16). We will share the message of the gospel of hope and salvation. We will live and act differently as we strive to live holy lives. And with the help of the Holy Spirit, we will testify to God's power and promise to those around us.

The Apostles' Teachings in the New Testament

In studying the signs of the Lord's return, we started with looking at the teachings of Jesus. As the ripples of time move further from the days Jesus lived on earth, the next thing we will look at are the teachings of those who studied under Jesus—the apostles. Jesus clarified the meaning of the scriptures to them and explained the meaning of his parables and prophecies. Next to Jesus himself, they had the clearest understanding of his teachings and prophecies.

There were twelve apostles including Judas Iscariot—Simon-Peter, Andrew, James, John, Philip, Bartholomew, Matthew, Thomas, James son of Alpheus, Simon the Zealot, and Jude-Thaddeus. Judas Iscariot hanged himself after betraying Jesus to the Roman authorities (Matthew 27:3-5). So, after Jesus's ascension, the apostles cast lots and replaced Judas Iscariot with Matthias.

In the New Testament, we have letters from four of the apostles— Matthew, Peter, John, and Jude. The first four gospels, which capture the life and teachings of Jesus, were written by two apostles—Matthew and John—and by two members of the early church—Mark and Luke, who documented the testimony of others who lived with and followed Jesus. Matthew's gospel is dedicated to capturing the life history and teachings of Jesus, parts of which were covered in the previous chapter.

Peter, John, and Jude wrote many letters as the early church was forming. Their letters clarified the teachings of Jesus and answered questions in the church. Peter's letters are in 1 and 2 Peter. John's letters are in 1 John, 2 John, 3 John, and Revelation. Jude's only recorded letter is in the book of Jude. There is also the book of James in the New Testament. However, most scholars believe this book was written by James, the half-brother of Jesus, not by either of the apostles named James.

Though writings of the other eight apostles are not included in today's New Testament, this does not mean they did not faithfully serve God. Just as we see today, believers have different spiritual gifts. With the unearthing of the Dead Sea Scrolls in twelve caves during 1946–1947, 1956, and 2017 along with writings used by the early church (that were not canonized and thus not used in the Bible), additional writings from the apostles and leaders of the early church were uncovered.

One other point of interest is that two of the men who wrote letters clarifying the end times, Peter and John, also sought out these answers for themselves at the foot of Jesus and witnessed his transfiguration. Do you remember the four apostles from the previous chapter who sought private audiences with Jesus on the Mount of Olives and asked him about the signs of his coming and the end of the age? They were Peter, Andrew, John, and James (Mark 13:3). Also, Peter, John, and James witnessed the transfiguration on the mountain with Elijah and Moses (Mark 9:2–4; Matthew 17:1–3).

> [2] After six days Jesus took Peter, James and John with him and led them up a high mountain, where they were all alone. There he was transfigured before them. [3] His clothes became dazzling white, whiter than anyone in the world could bleach them. [4] And there appeared before them Elijah and Moses, who were talking with Jesus. (Mark 9:2–4)

When we reviewed Jesus's teachings on the Mount of Olives, we considered the events these twelve apostles had witnessed during Jesus's ministry, events that led them to conclude he was the Messiah. Now let's consider the events that occurred after the Olivet Discourse and how these influenced the teaching to the churches that would come in the years following.

Jesus was crucified the week following the Olivet Discourse. Three days later, he arose from the dead. Peter and John raced to the empty tomb of Jesus when they heard from the women that he had risen (Luke 24:12; John 20:3–5). For the next forty days (Acts 1:3), the risen Jesus presented himself to his disciples, gave many convincing proofs that he was alive, and spoke about the kingdom of God. He also appeared to over 500 people (1 Corinthians 15:6).

Peter and John were commissioned by Jesus along with the other nine to go forth and make disciples of others after which they witnessed his ascension. The followers of Jesus received the power of the Holy Spirit on Pentecost Sunday (Acts 2:1–4) enabling them to preach, perform miracles, and fulfill Jesus's commission. At that point, the teachings of Jesus at the Mount of Olives were taking on a deeper meaning.

Peter's Teaching: The Timing of Jesus's Return

Just as Jesus prophesied, Peter became the rock upon which the church was built (Matthew 16:18). Peter gave many sermons in Acts including the one on Pentecost. Let's begin with his message in Acts 3:18–26 that pertains to the timing of Jesus's return.

> [18] But this is how God fulfilled what he had foretold through all the prophets, saying that his Messiah would suffer. [19] Repent, then, and turn to God, so that your sins may be wiped out, that times of refreshing may come from the Lord, [20] and that he may send the Messiah, who has been appointed for you—even Jesus. [21] Heaven must receive him until the time comes for

God to restore everything, as he promised long ago through his holy prophets. 22 For Moses said, "The Lord your God will raise up for you a prophet like me from among your own people; you must listen to everything he tells you.

23 Anyone who does not listen to him will be completely cut off from their people." 24 Indeed, beginning with Samuel, all the prophets who have spoken have foretold these days. 25 And you are heirs of the prophets and of the covenant God made with your fathers. He said to Abraham, "Through your offspring all peoples on earth will be blessed." 26 When God raised up his servant, he sent him first to you to bless you by turning each of you from your wicked ways. (Acts 3:18–26)

In this sermon, we learn that Jesus will be in heaven until the time comes for his return (v. 21). Until then, we should repent and turn from our wicked ways.

The period from the time Jesus ascended into heaven until "God restores everything" (Acts 3:21) is called the church age, the time between his first coming as Savior and his return in power and glory. This is the time we live in. In verse 24, we come to understand that the prophets have "foretold these days." We also see in verse 25 a reference to the Abrahamic covenant: "Through your offspring all peoples on earth will be blessed."

Let's look at an excerpt from 2 Peter, which was written about thirty years after Jesus's death. Peter died shortly after this letter was written in AD 67. In this passage, you see Peter answering the question, Why is Jesus's return taking longer than we expected? Let's take a look at his response in 2 Peter 3:3–18.

3 Above all, you must understand that in the last days scoffers will come, scoffing and following their own evil desires. 4 They will say, "Where is this 'coming' he

promised? Ever since our ancestors died, everything goes on as it has since the beginning of creation." [5] But they deliberately forget that long ago by God's word the heavens came into being and the earth was formed out of water and by water. [6] By these waters also the world of that time was deluged and destroyed. (2 Peter 3:3–6)

Four main points are made in this letter. First, Peter confirmed that we should not interpret the delay to mean Jesus had changed his mind about returning. There will be scoffers who will question his return, looking around and noticing that life goes on as it always has. However, we can be assured Jesus will return because God's word is trustworthy.

[7] By the same word the present heavens and earth are reserved for fire, being kept for the day of judgment and destruction of the ungodly ... [10] But the day of the Lord will come like a thief. The heavens will disappear with a roar; the elements will be destroyed by fire, and the earth and everything done in it will be laid bare ... [12] That day will bring about the destruction of the heavens by fire, and the elements will melt in the heat. [13] But in keeping with his promise we are looking forward to a new heaven and a new earth, where righteousness dwells. (2 Peter 3:7, 10, 12–13)

Second, at the end of the age, Jesus's return will be sudden and the earth will be destroyed by fire. Just as in the time of Noah, when humanity was ignoring God's prophesies and living unrepentant and confident that God would not judge them, destruction through the flood occurred suddenly. In the same way, Jesus will return suddenly.

[8] But do not forget this one thing, dear friends: With the Lord a day is like a thousand years, and a thousand years are like a day. [9] The Lord is not slow in keeping his promise, as some understand slowness. Instead he

is patient with you, not wanting anyone to perish, but everyone to come to repentance. (2 Peter 3:8–9)

Third, the delay in the Messiah's return reflects the patience of God and desire that none of his chosen perish. If we as believers are faithfully fulfilling Jesus's commission to go forth and make disciples, each day, we are partners with Jesus and the Holy Spirit in planting a harvest of new believers who are hearing the good news, are repenting and turning their hearts and minds over to Jesus, and who experience the gift of eternal life. Jesus has great love and compassion for the lost. Each day is an opportunity for continued prayer and the hope that more will be saved.

[11] Since everything will be destroyed in this way, what kind of people ought you to be? You ought to live holy and godly lives [12] as you look forward to the day of God and speed its coming … [14] So then, dear friends, since you are looking forward to this, make every effort to be found spotless, blameless and at peace with him … [17] Therefore, dear friends, since you have been forewarned, be on your guard so that you may not be carried away by the error of the lawless and fall from your secure position. [18] But grow in the grace and knowledge of our Lord and Savior Jesus Christ. To him be glory both now and forever! Amen. (2 Peter 3:11–12, 14, 17–18)

And fourth, Peter exhorted his fellow believers to "live holy and godly lives" (2 Peter 3:11), to "be on your guard that you may not be carried away by the error of lawlessness" (2 Peter 3:17), and to "grow in the grace and knowledge of our Lord" (2 Peter 3:18). Once again, we are reminded to live obedient and fruitful lives as we wait for the Lord's return. To live a holy life means to live a life "set apart for God," sacred and blameless. To live godly lives means to live in obedience to God's will and purpose, being careful not to adopt the ways of sinners.

As the psalm teaches,

> ¹ Blessed is the one who does not walk in step with the wicked or stand in the way that sinners take or sit in the company of mockers, ² but whose delight is in the law of the Lord, and who meditates on his law day and night. (Psalm 1:1–2)

And finally, Peter exhorted the church to grow in the grace and knowledge of our Lord, which is a deliberate effort on the part of believers to continually study God's Word and to be trained in righteousness.

John's Teaching: Recognizing False Messiahs

John's teachings related to the return of Jesus are in 1 John 2, 3 and 4. John's focus in these three letters is primarily on not being deceived by antichrists and a need to remain firm in faith.

> ¹⁵ Do not love the world or anything in the world. If anyone loves the world, love for the Father is not in them. ¹⁶ For everything in the world—the lust of the flesh, the lust of the eyes, and the pride of life—comes not from the Father but from the world. ¹⁷ The world and its desires pass away, but whoever does the will of God lives forever. ¹⁸ Dear children, this is the last hour; and as you have heard that the antichrist is coming, even now many antichrists have come. This is how we know it is the last hour. ¹⁹ They went out from us, but they did not really belong to us. For if they had belonged to us, they would have remained with us; but their going showed that none of them belonged to us.
>
> ²⁰ But you have an anointing from the Holy One, and all of you know the truth. ²¹ I do not write to you because you do not know the truth, but because you do know it and because no lie comes from the truth. ²² Who is the liar? It

is whoever denies that Jesus is the Christ. Such a person is the antichrist—denying the Father and the Son. [23] No one who denies the Son has the Father; whoever acknowledges the Son has the Father also. [24] As for you, see that what you have heard from the beginning remains in you. If it does, you also will remain in the Son and in the Father.

[25] And this is what he promised us—eternal life. [26] I am writing these things to you about those who are trying to lead you astray. [27] As for you, the anointing you received from him remains in you, and you do not need anyone to teach you. But as his anointing teaches you about all things and as that anointing is real, not counterfeit—just as it has taught you, remain in him. (1 John 2:15–27)

In 1 John 2:15–27, John told the church that we were in the last hour, that the Antichrist was coming, and that many antichrists have come. Jesus referred to these individuals as "false Messiahs" in the Olivet Discourse and indicated their presence was a sign that the end of the age is approaching. As with the other signs discussed, the volume and frequency of their appearance will increase as the time grows nearer.

John described antichrists as anyone who "denies that Jesus is the Christ" (1 John 2:22). Other indications that people are not following God is that they will be characterized by "the lust of the flesh, the lust of the eyes, and the pride of life" (1 John 2:16), that they will be "liars" (1 John 2:22), and that they would try to "lead you astray" (1 John 2:26).

[1] See what great love the Father has lavished on us, that we should be called children of God! And that is what we are! The reason the world does not know us is that it did not know him. [2] Dear friends, now we are children of God, and what we will be has not yet been made known. But we know that when Christ appears, we shall be like him, for we shall see him as he is. [3] All who have this hope in him purify themselves, just as he is pure. (1 John 3:1–3)

In 1 John 3, John wrote, "When Christ appears, we shall be like him." Much has been written about this section of scripture and what is meant by this expression. The Greek word used for "like" is *homoios*, which means similar in appearance or character.

Jesus was God, so no sin could be found in Him. Being like Christ means submitting to being transformed into his likeness. Romans 12:1–2 captures the spirit of this change.

> [1] Therefore, I urge you, brothers and sisters, in view of God's mercy, to offer your bodies as a living sacrifice, holy and pleasing to God—this is your true and proper worship. [2] Do not conform to the pattern of this world, but be transformed by the renewing of your mind. Then you will be able to test and approve what God's will is— his good, pleasing and perfect will. (Romans 12:1–2)

Another possibility is that what was being discussed in 1 John 3 was the transformation of our bodies to become like His—imperishable. In 1 Corinthians, Paul explains this change.

> Listen, I tell you a mystery: We will not all sleep, but we will all be changed—in a flash, in the twinkling of an eye, at the last trumpet. For the trumpet will sound, the dead will be raised imperishable, and we will be changed. For the perishable must clothe itself with the imperishable, and the mortal with immortality. When the perishable has been clothed with the imperishable, and the mortal with immortality, then the saying that is written will come true: "Death has been swallowed up in victory." (1 Corinthians 15:51–54)

Finally, in 1 John 4:1–3, John exhorted his fellow believers to "test the spirits" to confirm whether they were from God. Again, a simple test of whether the spirit acknowledges Jesus is from God will confirm the authenticity of the spirit. It is always astonishing to find individuals in the church who claim to be Christians yet deny the deity of Christ. This test is the first and most critical to ascertain the intent and allegiance of an individual.

> ¹ Dear friends, do not believe every spirit, but test the spirits to see whether they are from God, because many false prophets have gone out into the world. ² This is how you can recognize the Spirit of God: Every spirit that acknowledges that Jesus Christ has come in the flesh is from God, ³ but every spirit that does not acknowledge Jesus is not from God. This is the spirit of the antichrist, which you have heard is coming and even now is already in the world. (1 John 4:1–3)

Testing spirits may also involve listening to the words and observing the actions of an individual over time. It is not always easy to detect a false spirit at the beginning. I'm reminded of Jesus during his temptation in the desert by the devil. Satan was very crafty in his use of scripture, but he used it out of context to justify his purposes. Fortunately, Jesus was well versed in scripture and immediately recognized the deceit. Likewise, the ability to recognize false spirits may take some work on our part as we study scripture and grow in our understanding.

Jude's Teaching: Scoffers in the Church

In Jude, we are first reminded Jesus will be accompanied by the saints when he returns. Verse 14 reads, "See, the Lord is coming with thousands upon thousands of his holy ones." This same teaching that Jesus will not be alone as he returns in the sky is repeated in Revelation 19:14: "The armies of heaven were following him, riding on white horses and dressed in fine linen, white and clean."

> ¹⁴ Enoch, the seventh from Adam, prophesied about them:
> "See, the Lord is coming with thousands upon thousands

of his holy ones [15] to judge everyone, and to convict all of them of all the ungodly acts they have committed in their ungodliness, and of all the defiant words ungodly sinners have spoken against him." (Jude 14–15)

Second, we are told Jesus is coming to judge everyone (v. 15). There will be different judgments at the end of the age. However, the righteous and unrighteous alike will be held accountable for their actions. For those whose sins are not covered by the blood of Jesus, this will be a devastating time, a time when they realize that Jesus is real and that there is no room for defiance and sin in his kingdom.

[17] But, dear friends, remember what the apostles of our Lord Jesus Christ foretold. [18] They said to you, "In the last times there will be scoffers who will follow their own ungodly desires." [19] These are the people who divide you, who follow mere natural instincts and do not have the Spirit. (Jude 17–19)

Third, we are told there will be scoffers during the last times (v. 18). Jude described them as people who followed ungodly and natural desires, sought to divide the church, and did not have the Spirit in them. They sound very similar to those Peter encountered who were questioning the delayed timing of Jesus's return. "Above all, you must understand that in the last days scoffers will come, scoffing and following their own evil desires" (2 Peter 3:3).

[20] But you, dear friends, by building yourselves up in your most holy faith and praying in the Holy Spirit, [21] keep yourselves in God's love as you wait for the mercy of our Lord Jesus Christ to bring you to eternal life. [22] Be merciful to those who doubt; [23] save others by snatching them from the fire; to others show mercy, mixed with fear—hating even the clothing stained by corrupted flesh. (Jude 20–23)

In response to these scoffers, Jude exhorted his fellow believers to build up their faith, pray in the Holy Spirit, and have mercy on doubters. By building up their faith and praying, not only will the saints be better equipped to live righteous lives, but also, they will become more discerning.

Notice that the righteous are not called to judge the scoffers. This role of judge is reserved for Jesus. Instead, they are called to show mercy "mixed with fear" lest they also fall. They are exhorted to "save others by snatching them from the fire." Since only Jesus can save anyone, this refers to guiding the lost back to right thinking and correcting false teachings. It is with humility that believers realize that only Jesus "is able to keep you from stumbling and to present you before his glorious presence without fault and with great joy" (Jude 24).

Live Holy and Godly Lives

As we read the teachings of the apostles, we see that many of Jesus's teachings are repeated. Again, we are warned that Jesus's return will be unexpected and sudden and that we should be ready by living holy and godly lives. Peter and John remind us that Christians would be persecuted and that there would be false prophets. They reminded us of the persecution we will face and the need for us to show mercy and forgive others in the same way we hope the Lord will be merciful and forgive us on the day of judgment.

The apostles believed in Jesus's imminent return in their lifetime. This belief fueled their passion and urgency to share the message of the gospel. Jesus's words to stand firm in the face of persecution were fresh on their minds, and his promised return gave them courage and hope.

Bible Study Questions

1. **Jesus's Parting Words** (Acts 1:3–10)
   - It is not for you to _____ the times.
   - Jesus will return in the _____.

2. **Peter's Teaching—Timing of Jesus's return**
   * _____—the time between the first and second coming of Jesus (Acts 3:21).
   * Delay of Jesus second return (2 Peter 3:3–18).
     o Confirmed Jesus will return; God's _____ is trustworthy.
     o Destruction of earth at end of the age will be by _____.
     o Delay reflects _____ of God and desire that none of God's chosen _____.
     o Type of people we should be—live _____ and _____ lives; Be on guard; grow in _____ and _____ of the Lord.

3. **John's Teaching—Recognizing false messiahs**
   * We are in last hour; _____ is coming; many have come; will deny Jesus is the _____ (1 John 2:15–27).
   * When Jesus returns, we will be _____ Him (1 John 3:1–3).
   * _____ spirits to confirm whether from God (1 John 4:1–3).

4. **Jude's Teaching—Scoffers in the church** (Jude 14–22)
   * Jesus coming with _____.
   * Jesus is coming to _____ everyone.
   * There will be _____ in the last days.
   * Our response: build up our _____, _____, and have _____ on doubters.

Reflection

Are you living a holy and godly life growing in grace and knowledge of God?

CHAPTER 8

EARLY CHURCH TEACHINGS ON END TIMES

But you will receive power when the Holy Spirit comes
on you; and you will be my witnesses in Jerusalem, and in
all Judea and Samaria, and to the ends of the earth.
—Acts 1:8

As the apostles faithfully executed the Great Commission, the early church was formed in the first century following Jesus's resurrection. The New Testament records letters to the early church from approximately AD 30 to 90. The leaders of this body of believers known as the Way consisted of the apostles, men and women who had been discipled by them, and many new believers who received the message of the gospel. Some of them may have even witnessed the resurrected Jesus as stated in 1 Corinthians 15:6: "After that, he appeared to more than five hundred of the brothers and sisters at the same time, most of whom are still living, though some have fallen asleep."

Apart from the letters written by the apostles, the other letters that have been canonized as part of the New Testament were written primarily by Paul. However, some were also written by James, the brother of Jesus.

Paul did not start out as a follower of Jesus. Initially, he was a member of the Jewish sect called the Pharisees. Paul was zealous in his adherence to the laws of the Old Testament even to the point that he participated in persecuting the early Christians. Paul's conversion was an act of God recorded in Acts 9:1–19.

Once his change of heart had been validated by the apostles, he became as passionate a leader in the early church as he had been as a Pharisee. Barnabas "told them how Saul on his journey had seen the Lord and that the Lord had spoken to him, and how in Damascus he had preached fearlessly in the name of Jesus" (Acts 9:27). Paul's in-depth understanding of the scriptures helped him to explain how the teachings of Jesus fulfilled the teachings of the Old Testament.

As we saw in the teachings of the apostles in the previous chapters, the main questions of the early church pertaining to the return of Jesus were these.

- When will Jesus return?
- What events will precede that return?
- What events will accompany his return?
- How should we live as we wait?

1 Thessalonians 4 and 5—Timing of Jesus's Return

The first two letters written by Paul for the early church are 1 and 2 Thessalonians. Members of the church were looking for Jesus's return; the belief in his imminent return was at the front of every believer's mind. This was a difficult time for the church. Romans were cruel to Christians, and the Jewish establishment rejected the teaching that Jesus was the Messiah. The early church was anxious for deliverance.

Most of 1 Thessalonians looked at how Christians should behave. However, 1 Thessalonians 4:13–18 addresses resurrection and how living believers would be "caught up" in heaven with Jesus when he returned. The question was this: If a believer died before Jesus returned, would this cause him to lose all hope of sharing in the glorious reign of Christ? Paul's answer was the reassuring affirmation that the dead would be raised and share in the kingdom.

> ¹³ Brothers and sisters, we do not want you to be uninformed about those who sleep in death, so that you do not grieve like the rest of mankind, who have no hope. ¹⁴ For we believe that Jesus died and rose again, and so we believe that God will bring with Jesus those who have fallen asleep in him. ¹⁵ According to the Lord's word, we tell you that we who are still alive, who are left until the coming of the Lord, will certainly not precede those who have fallen asleep. ¹⁶ For the Lord himself will come down from heaven, with a loud command, with the voice of the archangel and with the trumpet call of God, and the dead in Christ will rise first. ¹⁷ After that, we who are still alive and are left will be caught up together with them in the clouds to meet the Lord in the air. And so we will be with the Lord forever. ¹⁸ Therefore encourage one another with these words. (1 Thessalonians 4:13–18)

As we look at these verses, we learn that when Jesus returns, he will resurrect the saints first, and then those who are alive will be "caught up" in the clouds. "And so we believe that God will bring with Jesus those who have fallen asleep in him" (1 Thessalonians 4:14). Those who have "fallen asleep" refer to the dead. Paul was very clear that "the dead in Christ will rise first" (1 Thessalonians 4:16). "After that, we who are still alive and are left will be caught up together with them in the clouds to meet the Lord in the air" (1 Thessalonians 4:17). The Greek word for "caught up" in verse 17 is *harpazo*, which means to "pluck," "pull up," or "take by force." This was consistent with the teaching of Jude, where we learned that the saints would accompany Jesus when he returned in the clouds. "See, the Lord is coming with thousands upon thousands of his holy ones" (Jude 14).

What is the timing of this event? That is the million-dollar question.

Some say Jesus will return, resurrect the dead, and lift up the saints to meet him at the beginning of the tribulation period. Others say this will occur when Jesus returns in power and glory at the end of the tribulation period. However, 1 Thessalonians 4 and 5 do not tell us anything about the timing but only that it will occur. What is important is that it will occur, not when it will occur.

The first part of 1 Thessalonians 5 confirmed that Jesus's return would be sudden and that we should be prepared for that day. Paul compared his return to the unwelcome and unexpected "thief in the night" (1 Thessalonians 5:2).

> [3] While people are saying, "Peace and safety," destruction will come on them suddenly, as labor pains on a pregnant woman, and they will not escape. [4] But you, brothers and sisters, are not in darkness so that this day should surprise you like a thief. [5] You are all children of the light and children of the day. We do not belong to the night or to the darkness. [6] So then, let us not be like others, who are asleep, but let us be awake and sober. (1 Thessalonians 5:3–6)

While "people are saying, 'Peace and safety', destruction will come on them suddenly" (1 Thessalonians 5:3). In contrast to the surprise that the rest of the world would experience, Jesus's return would not catch believers unaware since they were "children of the light" and Jesus had forewarned them.

Paul reminded believers that they should be "awake and sober" (1 Thessalonians 5:6). To ensure their faith was living and vital, he exhorted them to wear it daily by "putting on faith and love as a breastplate, and hope of salvation as a helmet" (1 Thessalonians 5:8). Paul frequently described faith using the analogy of armor. People in Israel encountered Roman soldiers in their day-to-day activities, so this comparison would resonate with them. In Paul's letters to the Ephesians, he used the same analogy with more detail.

> [13] Therefore put on the full armor of God, so that when the day of evil comes, you may be able to stand your ground, and after you have done everything, to stand. [14] Stand firm then, with the belt of truth buckled around your waist, with the breastplate of righteousness in place, [15] and with your feet fitted with the readiness that comes from the gospel of peace. [16] In addition to all this, take up the shield of faith, with which you can extinguish all the flaming arrows of the evil one. [17] Take the helmet of salvation and the sword of the Spirit, which is the word of God. (Ephesians 6:13–17)

This alertness and grounding in faith allows us to "live together with him" (1 Thessalonians 5:10). Jesus's death on the cross was not just so that we could live with him in heaven for eternity; it was also to liberate us from the spiritual death caused by our sins so that today, we could begin living the abundant lives God had planned for us. "I have come that they may have life, and have it to the full" (John 10:10).

2 Thessalonians 1—Day of Judgment

In the first chapter of 2 Thessalonians, Paul discussed the suddenness of the return of Jesus and the judgment of unbelievers. The church in Thessalonica was reminded that God was just and that there would be judgment for those who rejected the Messiah.

> [5] All this is evidence that God's judgment is right, and as a result you will be counted worthy of the kingdom of God, for which you are suffering. [6] God is just: He will pay back trouble to those who trouble you [7] and give relief to you who are troubled, and to us as well. This will happen when the Lord Jesus is revealed from heaven in blazing fire with his powerful angels. [8] He will punish those who do not know God and do not obey the

gospel of our Lord Jesus. [9] They will be punished with everlasting destruction and shut out from the presence of the Lord and from the glory of his might [10] on the day he comes to be glorified in his holy people and to be marveled at among all those who have believed. This includes you, because you believed our testimony to you. [11] With this in mind, we constantly pray for you, that our God may make you worthy of his calling, and that by his power he may bring to fruition your every desire for goodness and your every deed prompted by faith. (2 Thessalonians 1:5–13)

One of the common misconceptions about judgment is the law on which it is based. We are inclined to base judgment decisions on contemporary perception, morals, and understanding, which are constantly evolving. Yet God's nature and character is immutable, which means he doesn't change. And the basis for God's judgment are standards of righteousness and truth that have been in place since the beginning of time. The fundamental requirements of a just God are outlined in verse 8—knowing God and obeying the gospel of the Lord.

Paul made a few key points regarding judgment. First, "God's judgment is right" (2 Thessalonians 1:6). This means that God does not make mistakes when it comes to judging us. He knows our hearts and thoughts, and the judgment he metes out will be deserved and accurate. Second, Paul wrote, "God is just" (2 Thessalonians 1:6). This speaks to the character of God. God is inherently pure and without sin. As such, he is able to be totally just and unswayed by deception and lies.

Third, judgment will occur when Jesus returns with "his powerful angels" (2 Thessalonians 1:7). And fourth, judgment consists of "everlasting destruction" for those who are found unworthy (2 Thessalonians 1:5–11).

> There will be a day of accountability that we are all destined to face. Whether we choose to believe it or not does not change the reality.

The reality of ultimate judgment and accountability before God should "shake us to our boots." There will be a day of accountability that we are all destined to face. Whether we choose to believe it or not does not change the reality. Paul understood this and was moved to fervent prayer for his fellow Christians that they would be found "worthy" before God and that their lives would "bring to fruition your every desire for goodness and your every deed prompted by faith" (2 Thessalonians 1:11). Likewise, we should be in fervent prayer for one another.

2 Thessalonians 2—Man of Lawlessness

In 2 Thessalonians 2:1–12, false teachers had crept into the church and were beginning to distort the teachings around the timing of Jesus's return.

> [1] Concerning the coming of our Lord Jesus Christ and our being gathered to him, we ask you, brothers and sisters, [2] not to become easily unsettled or alarmed by the teaching allegedly from us—whether by a prophecy or by word of mouth or by letter—asserting that the day of the Lord has already come. [3] Don't let anyone deceive you in any way, for that day will not come until the rebellion occurs and the man of lawlessness is revealed, the man doomed to destruction. [4] He will oppose and will exalt himself over everything that is called God or is worshiped, so that he sets himself up in God's temple,

proclaiming himself to be God. [5] Don't you remember that when I was with you I used to tell you these things?

[6] And now you know what is holding him back, so that he may be revealed at the proper time. [7] For the secret power of lawlessness is already at work; but the one who now holds it back will continue to do so till he is taken out of the way. [8] And then the lawless one will be revealed, whom the Lord Jesus will overthrow with the breath of his mouth and destroy by the splendor of his coming. [9] The coming of the lawless one will be in accordance with how Satan works. He will use all sorts of displays of power through signs and wonders that serve the lie, [10] and all the ways that wickedness deceives those who are perishing. They perish because they refused to love the truth and so be saved. [11] For this reason God sends them a powerful delusion so that they will believe the lie [12] and so that all will be condemned who have not believed the truth but have delighted in wickedness. (2 Thessalonians 2:1–12)

A serious concern was raised by the church "concerning the coming of our Lord Jesus Christ and our being gathered to him" (2 Thessalonians 2:1). Some teachers were saying that Jesus's return had already occurred and that these folks had missed out! I don't know if you have ever had that worry, but I recall years ago when I was in my twenties, I showed up to church one Sunday and the parking lot was empty. I scratched my head and asked myself, *Oh no! Did the rapture come and I missed it?* As I shook the morning cobwebs out of my head, it finally dawned on me that daylight savings had come, not the Messiah, and I had forgotten to adjust my clock. But you can imagine the angst if you are a believer and you are thinking Jesus did not count you worthy.

Paul immediately set out to alleviate their concerns. Don't "become easily unsettled or alarmed" (2 Thessalonians 2:2), and don't "let anyone deceive you" (2 Thessalonians 2:3) he cautioned the body of believers.

They had not missed the return of Jesus. Paul pointed them back to the teachings and prophecy of Jesus regarding the events preceding his return.

Jesus's return will not occur "until the rebellion occurs and the man of lawlessness is revealed" (2 Thessalonians 2:3). We've seen this same individual also referred to as the "abomination that causes desolation" (Matthew 24:15) and the "Antichrist" (1 John 2:18). Verse 3 identified the rebellion that would occur in conjunction with the revelation of the "man of lawlessness." Footnotes in my Bible indicate that this rebellion refers to "an aggressive and climatic revolt against God that will prepare the way for the appearance"[30] of the man of lawlessness. In Matthew, Jesus prophesied that this man would "stand in the holy place" and that those in Judea should "flee" (Matthew 24:15–16). Paul added that he would "oppose and exalt himself over everything that is called God and is worshiped" and that he would proclaim "himself to be God" (2 Thessalonians 2:4).

Starting in verse 6, Paul wrote the "man of lawlessness" was being held back. The Greek word for "held back" is *katecho*, which means to "hold down," "keep," or "restrain." From this definition, some label the power that is holding him back as the restrainer.

There are several theories as to who the restrainer is. The most popular theories are that the restrainer is a reference to the role of the Holy Spirit. Others believe that this refers to the church's influence on society. Either way, God alone knows the timing of these events, and the man of lawlessness will be "revealed at the proper time" (2 Thessalonians 2:6).

When Jesus does return, he will "overthrow" the man of lawlessness and "destroy" him (2 Thessalonians 2:8). A similar prophecy is confirmed by John in Revelation, where in his vision the "beast was captured, and with it the false prophet who had performed the signs on its behalf and both were thrown alive into the fiery lake of burning sulfur" (Revelation 19:20).

However, during the time this man is in power, he will use "all sorts of displays of power through signs and wonders" to deceive those who are "perishing." Jesus prophesied that after the "abomination that causes desolation" was seen standing in the holy place, there would be false messiahs with signs and wonders (Matthew 24:24). These displays of power are not from God; they will be satanic in origin. They will serve to impress and deceive those who are not grounded in the truth of the scriptures. Their increased wickedness and rejection of God will lead to a "depraved mind" (Romans 1:28). "They perish because they refused to love the truth and so be saved" (2 Thessalonians 2:10). The result will be that those who reject God "will be condemned" (2 Thessalonians 2:12).

In contrast to the sad destiny for those who are deceived, believers are called to "share in the glory of our Lord Jesus Christ" (2 Thessalonians 2:14). Paul exhorted believers to "stand firm and hold fast to the teachings we passed on to you" (2 Thessalonians 2:15). Then, Jesus, who has and will continue to love us, gives us "eternal encouragement and good hope" and strengthens us for "every good deed and word" (2 Thessalonians 2:16–17).

In 2 Thessalonians 3, believers are exhorted to pray and be disciplined, both of which are essential in the last days. These disciplines will enable them to stand firm in faith. Notice that as we read these scriptures, we learn that following Christ is not passive. Our faith is intended to be exercised through understanding and studying the scriptures, prayer, and obedience. We should actively live for God or risk being found unworthy, weak in our minds and bodies or being deceived by the "man of lawlessness" and those who follow him.

Rapture

A topic often discussed is whether believers who are living during the tribulation will be raptured in advance of Jesus's return as king. To understand the interpretation of scriptures regarding this, we need to briefly review different viewpoints concerning the millennium.

You will not find the word *millennium* in the scriptures, but it is derived from the Latin words *milo,* "thousand," and *annus,* "year"; millennium refers to a thousand years. This term derives from the time period of the thousand-year rule of Jesus referenced in Revelation 20.

> [2] He seized the dragon, that ancient serpent, who is the devil, or Satan, and bound him for a thousand years. [3] He threw him into the Abyss, and locked and sealed it over him, to keep him from deceiving the nations anymore until the thousand years were ended … [4] And I saw the souls of those who had been beheaded because of their testimony about Jesus and because of the word of God. They had not worshiped the beast or its image and had not received its mark on their foreheads or their hands. They came to life and reigned with Christ a thousand years. (Revelation 20:2–4)

Three different outlooks regarding the interpretation of this time period of "a thousand years" (Revelation 20:4) and events leading up to the millennium have evolved over time in the Christian church. Some believers interpret the millennial time frame literally, which include the pre- and postmillennialists. Others interpret it to be symbolic, which include amillennialists.

The amillennialists (realized millennialists) interpret the millennial period symbolically and do not think that it literally refers to a thousand years; they believe Christians are already in the millennium period. In this interpretation, Satan was bound when Christ came the first time. They believe that the present church age will continue until Christ's return and that the church as represented by the body of believers will share in the tribulation period. They also expect there to be one resurrection of both believers and unbelievers that will be followed by judgments and rewards. They do not believe there will be a separate rapture of believers prior to Christ's return. Some of the churches that hold to this view today are Eastern and Oriental Orthodox Churches, the Roman Catholic Church, and some Protestant denominations such as Church of Christ. (This is not an exhaustive list of churches that hold this view. Also, in this group, some have embraced components of the premillennialist view.)

Postmillennialists believe the progress of the gospel and the growth of the church will gradually bring in a millennial age of peace and righteousness. The literal meaning of postmillennialism is that Jesus will return after the millennium, which means that at Christ's return, the general resurrection and judgment would immediately occur and then Christ would usher in the eternal state of the new heavens and earth.

Further, postmillennialists do not teach that there will be a separate rapture of believers prior to Christ's return; they believe there will be one resurrection and judgment for both believers and unbelievers. According to Beth Moore, "Two world wars and the tumult of the 20th century effectively killed this optimistic view."[31]

Even today, we see wars all around us, which cause us to question whether it is possible for people to ever live in an age of peace on their own. While many have been saved through the preaching of the gospel all around the world, unabated evil seems to continually disrupt the few advancements we make toward peace. While this is not a widely held point of view, postmillennialism has become a key tenet in a recent movement known as Christian reconstructionism.

Premillennialists interpret the thousand years to be Christ's physical kingdom set up on earth after his return. In this interpretation, the church age will occur before the onset of the millennial period referenced in Revelation 20:4. However, premillennialists divide into two very different models of understanding the future—historic traditionalists and dispensationalists.

According to Beth Moore, both models of premillennialism agree about the events at the end of the thousand years. After the final judgment, believers will enter the eternal state.[32] These events would include,

- Satan being "set free from the bottomless pit" for a short time,
- Satan joining forces with any residual unbelievers who have "submitted outwardly to Christ's reign but have inwardly been seething in rebellion against him,"
- a great battle in which Christ and his army would be victorious and Satan would be defeated once and for all,

- Christ raising "from the dead all the unbelievers who have died throughout history,"
- and unbelievers standing "before him for final judgment."

Historic (traditional) premillennialists expect the church to go through the tribulation period. According to Beth Moore,

> After that time of tribulation at the end of the church age, Christ will return to earth to establish a millennial kingdom. When he comes back, believers who have died will be raised from the dead, their bodies will be reunited with their spirits, and these believers will reign with Christ on earth for one thousand years.[33]

This viewpoint dates to the early church and the first century following Christ's death and resurrection. The early church anticipated going through the tribulation period and encouraged perseverance and courage during the periods of time saints were persecuted with the promise of ultimate resurrection and reunion with the Lord.

Premillennial dispensationalism is the most recent of the millennial viewpoints and emerged in the nineteenth century. Again Beth Moore explains,

> Dispensationalists understand Israel to be a people of God distinct from the church. The tribulation period, and particularly the millennium, fulfills God's promises and dealing with the nation of Israel. The rapture of the church happens either before the seven-year tribulation period or at the three and one-half year midpoint. At the rapture the church is taken to heaven leaving the judgments and promises of God to fall on unrepentant humanity and national Israel.[34]

So while all views agree Jesus will return, there is disagreement as to the timing of when believers will be caught up with him and the interpretation of his thousand-year reign.

You will not find the word *rapture* used in the scripture; it comes from the Latin root *raptus*, meaning "seized," "kidnapped," "snatched," and the like. The Greek word closest to this meaning is *harpazo*, which is used in 1 Thessalonians 4:17 and translated as "caught up." "After that, we who are still alive and are left will be caught up together with them in the clouds to meet the Lord in the air." However, according to this scripture, the only mention of the timing of this event is that it will occur when the Lord returns.

Revelation 3:10 is used to justify the idea that believers will be spared the tribulation, though these words were given specifically to the church of Philadelphia. The question here would be if the church at Philadelphia represents all believers and if the "hour of trial" refers to the tribulation period, neither of which is clearly supported by the text: "Since you have kept my command to endure patiently, I will also keep you from the hour of trial that is going to come on the whole world to test the inhabitants of the earth" (Revelation 3:10).

Another section of scripture used to support the viewpoint of a separate rapture of believers is Luke 17:26–30, in which Jesus compared the coming of the kingdom of God to the "days of Noah" and the "days of Lot." In both cases, the "righteous" were removed or secured before the judgment of God fell.

> [26] Just as it was in the days of Noah, so also will it be in the days of the Son of Man. [27] People were eating, drinking, marrying and being given in marriage up to the day Noah entered the ark. Then the flood came and destroyed them all. [28] It was the same in the days of Lot. People were eating and drinking, buying and selling, planting and building. [29] But the day Lot left Sodom, fire and sulfur rained down from heaven and destroyed them all. [30] It will be just like this on the day the Son of Man is revealed. (Luke 17:26–30)

As the parable continues, in Luke 17:34, Jesus stated, "I tell you, on that night two people will be in one bed; one will be taken and the other left." The word *taken* comes from the Greek word *paralambano*, which literally means to "receive" or "take with." In contemporary books and movies, the idea of believers being taken unexpectedly during this period of tribulation is depicted as people disappearing suddenly from their daily activities leaving clothes, possessions and confused families behind. Another way to understand this scripture is to interpret it as divided families and neighbors as some follow and receive Jesus as Lord and others reject him.

Finally, another set of scriptures used to support the rapture are 2 Thessalonians 2:1–3. The application of this verse to the rapture is not as obvious since it is inferred by our being "gathered to him" (v. 1), which will not happen until the "man of lawlessness is revealed" (v. 3).

> [1] Concerning the coming of our Lord Jesus Christ and our being gathered to him, we ask you, brothers and sisters, [2] not to become easily unsettled or alarmed by the teaching allegedly from us—whether by a prophecy or by word of mouth or by letter—asserting that the day of the Lord has already come. [3] Don't let anyone deceive you in any way, for that day will not come until the rebellion occurs and the man of lawlessness is revealed, the man doomed to destruction. (2 Thessalonians 2:1–3)

Most scriptures pointing to a rapture before the tribulation period can be interpreted various ways, so it is difficult to be dogmatic about this being an event separate from Jesus's final return. But we can be assured that if we are living when Christ returns, we will be caught up in the air with Him.

2 Timothy 3—False Messiahs and Persecution of Saints

In 2 Timothy 3, Paul warned us again of the degeneration of humanity during the end times. As humanity is given over to the control of sin in their lives, it will reveal itself in immoral character and loss of compassion. Let's look first at 2 Timothy 3:1–9.

> ¹ But mark this: There will be terrible times in the last days. ² People will be lovers of themselves, lovers of money, boastful, proud, abusive, disobedient to their parents, ungrateful, unholy, ³ without love, unforgiving, slanderous, without self-control, brutal, not lovers of the good, ⁴ treacherous, rash, conceited, lovers of pleasure rather than lovers of God— ⁵ having a form of godliness but denying its power. Have nothing to do with such people. ⁶ They are the kind who worm their way into homes and gain control over gullible women, who are loaded down with sins and are swayed by all kinds of evil desires, ⁷ always learning but never able to come to a knowledge of the truth. ⁸ Just as Jannes and Jambres opposed Moses, so also these teachers oppose the truth. They are men of depraved minds, who, as far as the faith is concerned, are rejected. ⁹ But they will not get very far because, as in the case of those men, their folly will be clear to everyone. (2 Timothy 3:1–9)

In this section, Paul described the state that depraved and godless people would find themselves in. The litany of adjectives in verses 2–4 condemns their character. They are described as lovers of self, money, and pleasure instead of being lovers of good and God. It seems that just about every negative adjective Paul could think of was attached to these insincere, ungodly people—boastful, proud, abusive, disobedient, ungrateful, unholy, unloving, unforgiving, slanderous, out of control, brutal, treacherous, rash, and conceited.

Can you imagine that anyone would want to follow or even be

in the proximity of such people? Yet they are masters of deceit. They have a form of godliness, which refers to having the outer semblance of godliness without its spiritual dynamic. For all their appearance of being righteous, in truth, they "deny its power," learn but never "come to a knowledge of the truth," and even actively "oppose the truth" (2 Timothy 3:5, 7, and 8). We are told to "have nothing to do with such people" (2 Timothy 35).

> They have a form of godliness, which refers to having the outer semblance of godliness without its spiritual dynamic.

Paul compared the opposition to truth of these depraved men to "Jannes and Jambres" (2 Timothy 3:8). These names do not appear in the Old Testament and may not be well known today. However, in certain early Christian writings Jannes and Jambres were "Egyptian magicians who performed counterfeit miracles in opposition to Moses"[35] (Exodus 7:11, 22). Likewise, those who "oppose the truth" were men who performed counterfeit miracles in an effort to distort the truth and deceive believers.

In 2 Timothy 3:12–13, Paul wrote, "In fact, everyone who wants to live a godly life in Christ Jesus will be persecuted, while evildoers and impostors will go from bad to worse, deceiving and being deceived."

Jesus likewise warned his followers of persecution: "Then you will be handed over to be persecuted and put to death, and you will be hated by all nations because of me" (Matthew 24:9). Satan "prowls around like a roaring lion looking for someone to devour" (1 Peter 5:8). Satan's domain is this world, and as such, it is no surprise that the enemy of God will seek out and try to hurt and persecute those who seek to follow God in righteousness. Unfortunately, some in the church "will abandon their faith and follow deceiving spirits and things taught by demons" (1 Timothy 4:1–2).

The best defense against Satan is a good offense. Believers are to know "the Holy Scriptures, which are able to make you wise for salvation through faith in Christ Jesus" (2 Timothy 3:15). After all, all "scripture is God-breathed." Scripture is "useful for teaching, rebuking, correcting and training in righteousness" and will equip us "for every good work" (2 Timothy 3:16–17).

Many Christians have memorized these verses from Timothy as they reflected on the importance of studying God's Word. But is also worthwhile to consider this scripture in the context of the end times. We are reminded that understanding and knowing God's Word is essential to being able to stand firm against persecution and false teachings.

Deep Roots

Paul, a Jew, turned out to be an excellent messenger for the early church. He was deeply rooted in the knowledge of Old Testament teachings; his zealous love for God gave him strength and courage. Though he faced many obstacles, he faithfully shared the message of the gospel and taught many new believers the basic tenets of their faith.

Each generation of Christians who follow Jesus, his apostles, and leaders in the early church have a responsibility to carry on the message of the gospel and the teachings of the scriptures. Each of us is called to become deeply rooted in the understanding of the truth found in the scriptures so we can faithfully disciple the generations that follow until Jesus's return.

Bible Study Questions

1. **1 Thessalonians 4–5—Timing of Jesus's Return**
   - When Jesus returns, first, he will _____ the saints and second, those who are alive will be _____ in the clouds (1 Thessalonians 4:13–18)

- Return _____; be awake and sober; put on _____ of God (1 Thessalonians 5:1–11).

2. **2 Thessalonians 1—Day of Judgment**
   - God is _____; judgment will occur when Jesus returns with his _____; judgment of

   _____

   (2 Thessalonians 1:5–11).

3. **2 Thessalonians 2—Man of Lawlessness**
   - Don't be _____ that you have _____ the return of Jesus (2 Thessalonians 2:1–2).
   - Jesus will not come until prophecy concerning _____ is fulfilled (2 Thessalonians 2:3–4).
   - _____ is holding back the man of lawlessness for the time being (2 Thessalonians 2:5–8).
   - Deceives those who are _____ (2 Thessalonians 2:9–12).

4. **2 Timothy 3—False Messiahs; Persecution of Saints**
   - Form of _____, but denying its power; oppose the _____ (2 Timothy 3:1–9).
   - Scriptures are _____; make you _____ for salvation (2 Timothy 3:10–17).

Reflection

It is easy to be deceived by false teachings that appear to follow the scriptures but distort its teaching. What are you doing to prevent yourself from being a victim of deceit?

PART 3

ARE YOU READY?

CHAPTER 9

PREPARING FOR THE LORD'S RETURN

Be very careful, then, how you live—not as unwise but as wise,
making the most of every opportunity, because the days are evil.
—Ephesians 5:15–16

Just the sheer magnitude of information in the scripture regarding the
end times tells us this period is important. As Christians wait for the
imminent return of Jesus and that epic day of judgment, we have an
important part to play in the latter days.

How Then Should We Live?

As we study the scriptures, we are exhorted to live godly lives. In the
Old Testament, God provided his commands through his prophets and
the early leaders of his people. Jesus gave us guidelines in his teaching
as to how we should be living as the signs begin appearing around us
and the days draw nearer to his return. Leaders in the early church
reinforced both the teachings of the Old Testament and Jesus providing
additional clarity.

If you are still unsure how you should be living, you can ask God
directly for clarity. As it says in Mark 12:30, God wants you to love
him "with all your heart and with all your soul and with all your mind
and with all your strength." To love God with your mind implies a

thoughtful learning and understanding of the scriptures, which means you will have questions. Just as God did not rebuke the disciples for asking him these questions, he will not rebuke you when you ask questions with a genuine desire to understand.

The disciples of Jesus provided an example when they went to him privately to talk with him on the Mount of Olives (Matthew 24:3). Jesus was happy to answer his trusted and close followers. Also, we are encouraged to "pray without ceasing" (1 Thessalonians 5:17, KJV). This spiritual exercise of constantly bringing our concerns and needs to God is essential to building trust, faith, and understanding: "The prayer of a righteous person is powerful and effective" (James 5:16).

In review of the teachings on the end times, we find direction on living through wars, famines, pestilence, false messiahs, the leader who will emerge and cause desolation in the holy place, persecution, and heavenly unrest in epic proportions. Our earth and people all around us will be reeling from the instability and constant attack on their persons, emotions, and senses. As Christians, we will endure these times as we faithfully keep our eyes on Jesus.

Don't Be Deceived

In the midst of false messiahs and teachers, Christians are warned to watch out and pay attention so they won't be deceived. They will have to exercise discernment and understanding of the scriptures and test the messengers who deliver them. "Jesus said to them: 'Watch out that no one deceives you. Many will come in my name, claiming, "I am he," and will deceive many'" (Mark 13:5–6).

So how do we avoid becoming deceived? In 2 Peter 2, we find a systematic review of the character traits of these individuals that will help us distinguish between counterfeit and authentic messages. These false prophets will,

- "Secretly introduce destructive heresies" (2 Peter 2:1),
- bring "truth into disrepute" (2 Peter 2:2) by their depraved conduct and by suppressing it (Romans 1:1),
- exploit people with "false arguments and twisted doctrine" (2 Peter 2:3),
- "blaspheme in matters they do not understand" (2 Peter 2:12) thus proving themselves unreasonable and disrespectful of authority,
- enslave people through their depraved empty boastful words and entice them by "appealing to their lustful desires of the flesh" (2 Peter 2:18), and
- "never stop sinning" (2 Peter 2:14).

By watching for these traits, we will be able to identify false prophets, be wary of their messages, and avoid following them.

Don't Be Alarmed

As our world succumbs to wars, rumors of wars, famines, pestilence, and devastating natural events, it is almost with a sense of reluctant acceptance that all three gospels state "Such things must happen, but the end is still to come" (Matthew 24:6).

Jesus simply instructs his follows to not "be alarmed." We should not panic or be distraught by the unraveling of nations around us or as the security of food supplies and health seem to totter, or even as heavenly events cause our earth to shake. As Christians, our perspective of global events should be firmly planted in the knowledge of God's sovereignty and the promise of the Messiah's return. In a calm, confident response to these events will lie an opportunity to show the heart of Jesus through compassion, mercy, and love.

> In a calm, confident response to these events will lie an opportunity to show the heart of Jesus through compassion, mercy, and love.

Stand Firm in Faith

Threats of persecution may come from many sources—religious leaders, politicians, evil dynasties, family, or even other believers. Regardless of the source, we need to walk firmly in faith.

> [9] You must be on your guard. You will be handed over to the local councils and flogged in the synagogues. On account of me you will stand before governors and kings as witnesses to them ... [12] Brother will betray brother to death, and a father his child. Children will rebel against their parents and have them put to death. [13] Everyone will hate you because of me, but the one who stands firm to the end will be saved. (Mark 13:9, 12)

> When we feel most afraid, when our lives and our freedom are in jeopardy, the Holy Spirit will be strengthening us and equipping us to stand firm.

In Matthew 10, Jesus told us not to worry about what we will say if we are arrested or brought before authorities. The Holy Spirit will be holding us up at that time and will give us the words to speak. In response to the persecution, Jesus told us to stand firm in faith. To those who are faithful, he promises salvation. When we feel most afraid, when our lives and our freedom are in jeopardy, the Holy Spirit will be strengthening us and equipping us to stand firm.

¹⁹ But when they arrest you, do not worry about what to
say or how to say it. At that time you will be given what
to say, ²⁰ for it will not be you speaking, but the Spirit of
your Father speaking through you. (Matthew 10:19–20)

Revelation promises those churches that remain faithful and
overcome the persecution the right to eat from the tree of life (Revelation
2:7), the guarantee to not be hurt by the second death (Revelation 2:11),
and the privilege of being a pillar in the temple of God for eternity
(Revelation 3:12).

Flee to Safety

To those unfortunate enough to be in Jerusalem when the
abomination that causes desolation marches in, Jesus gives a simple
order—flee! "…then let those who are in Judea flee to the mountains.
Let no one on the housetop go down to take anything out of the house.
Let no one in the field go back to get their cloak" (Matthew 24:16–18).

These will be dangerous times in Jerusalem, and many will die
by the sword. In this case, hiding and seeking safety for you and your
family is the right and urgent response.

Be on Guard

The final days will witness an increase in demonic activity, powers,
and deception. In addition to not being deceived, Christians are warned
to be on guard: "For false messiahs and false prophets will appear and
perform great signs and wonders to deceive, if possible, even the elect"
(Matthew 24:24).

It will not be enough in these days to passively be on the defensive.
Similar to those in Jerusalem who are fleeing for their lives, Christians
around the world will need to be in a heightened stage of self-protection
and awareness.

Be Ready; Watch

In the parables from the Olivet Discourse—of Noah and Lot, of the thief and the obedient servants, and of the ten virgins—Jesus gave a stern warning to keep watch for his return and be ready. Since no one knows the timing of his return, we are all exhorted to be ready. Part of being ready is being obedient, doing what God has commanded us to do, living righteously, being merciful, doing good to others, and growing in faith.

Be My Witnesses

Jesus commanded Christians to be his witnesses. In Acts 1:8, he told his followers, "You will receive power when the Holy Spirit comes on you; and you will be my witnesses in Jerusalem, and in all Judea and Samaria, and to the ends of the earth." Being a witness means testifying to the works and life of Jesus and to the power he has to save us.

In the parables following Jesus's discussion of the end times on the Mount of Olives, he compared believers to obedient servants who wisely invest the riches left by the master, to wise bridesmaids who were ready for the groom's return, and to sheep who followed their shepherd's example by being compassionate. It was no accident that these parables accompanied the signs of the end times. To follow Jesus evokes a transformed lifestyle as we fully understand the great work of salvation and the gift of eternal life. It demands obedience as we submit to him as Lord of our lives.

Make Disciples

After his resurrection, Jesus commanded his disciples to make disciples of all nations. This is referred to the Great Commission. Just as Jesus said that one of the signs preceding his return was the spread of the gospel to all nations, these scriptures direct Jesus's followers and later, those who become their disciples, that they have a responsibility to baptize and teach others what it means to live as Christians as we approach the end of the age. "Therefore go and make disciples of all nations, baptizing them in the name of the Father and of the Son and of the Holy Spirit, and teaching them to obey everything I have commanded you. And surely I am with you always, to the very end of the age" (Matthew 28:19-20)

As We Wait for His Return ...

Jesus told his followers he would go away and come back. In the parables of gold, Jesus alluded to a master going on a journey and returning (Matthew 25:14–15, 19). Also, in John 14:28–29 and John 16:19–20, 28, Jesus taught that he would go away and return. At the time of his return, the grief and suffering of his followers would be turned to joy as Jesus overcomes this world.

> [19] Jesus saw that they wanted to ask him about this, so he said to them, "Are you asking one another what I meant when I said, 'In a little while you will see me no more, and then after a little while you will see me'? [20] Very truly I tell you, you will weep and mourn while the world rejoices. You will grieve, but your grief will turn to joy." (John 16:19–20)

Note the simplicity and directness of Jesus's response to the disciples' questions. Jesus's way is true and straight; we can simply believe Him. Consider some of his commands to his followers. "Believe" and you will be saved (Acts 16:31). "Ask" for wisdom and Jesus will give it to you (James 1:5). "Cast" your cares on Him (1 Peter 5:7). "Don't worry" about your life because God knows your need (Matthew 6:25–32). If you love me, you will "obey" me (John 14:15). These are simple actions—believe, ask, cast, don't worry, and obey.

The same is true as we consider his exhortations for how we should live as we wait for his return—be ready, watch, be on guard, stand firm, don't be alarmed, be my witnesses, and make disciples. Let us pray that our actions will be found worthy before the Lord and that we will be able to stand before Him in judgment.

Bible Study Questions

Christian Responses

1. False messiahs—_____ that no one deceives you.

2. Wars, unrest among nations, famines, pestilence, earthquakes, and heavenly signs—Don't be _____.

3. Persecution of saints and gospel spread to nations—Stand _____ in faith.

4. Abomination that causes desolation in holy place—Those in Judea _____ to the mountains.

5. False messiahs and prophets—Don't believe lies; be on _____.

6. Be my _____; make _____.

CHAPTER 10

A TIME TO CHOOSE

For in the gospel the righteousness of God is revealed—a
righteousness that is by faith from first to last, just as
it is written: "The righteous will live by faith."
—Romans 1:17

Why do believers need to study the events of the end times? Why did God give visions to the prophets of the Old Testament? Why did Jesus warn his followers of the signs leading up to his return?

When God was speaking with the Israelites through the prophets, he was telling them that their choices between righteousness and sin mattered. If they sinned, there would be consequences, but if they were righteous, God would bless them.

When Jesus was speaking with his followers, he was also telling them that how they lived mattered. They were exhorted to be ready and to live righteously, courageously, and with faith.

We can be assured that the events of the end time will happen. God has foreseen these times and passed on these visions to his people by means of his prophets. What matters now is how we live between today and Jesus's return. Will we choose God? Will we live with courage and conviction? Or will we be foolish and follow the ways of this world?

The apostles and the early church were motivated by their hope in the imminent return of Jesus. This is understandable given they had heard the teachings of Jesus and witnessed him after his resurrection from the dead. They were enthused and amazed by his power. Also, persecution by the Romans and Jewish leaders was sometimes unbearable. The early church was hopeful that Jesus would come soon and rescue them from persecution.

In Acts 1:7, Jesus's last teaching to his disciples was, "It is not for you to know the times or dates the Father has set by his own authority." Jesus sought to refocus their thinking. Instead of worrying about when he would return, he wanted them to concentrate on living righteous, obedient, and spirit-filled lives. The belief in Jesus's imminent return inspired early Christians to live in a state of constant readiness knowing Jesus could return any day.

Almost 2,000 years later, we look at the signs prophesied by Jesus still watching for and anticipating that his return is imminent. We are seeing a number of events today that lead us to believe Jesus's return is very close. Jesus could return in our lifetime, tomorrow, or in a future generation. But like Peter and the early church experienced, as the years go by and Jesus doesn't return to reign, many will question the accuracy of this prophecy or its literal fulfillment.

Today, Christians respond to this delay in different ways. They may try to reexplain it by watering down the scriptures (e.g., he didn't mean his return literally ... or Jesus meant that the spirit of Christ will come versus his literal return). Or they may predict his return will be so far in the future that they are tempted to become complacent in their Christian walk. Or perhaps they just get caught up in material and secular concerns and live for the moment.

> The loss of a sense of urgency, readiness, and faith in our response to Jesus's promise to return in power and glory is detrimental to our Christian walk.

While it may be difficult to interpret the timing of Jesus's return and what it might look like, we have to be cautious that delays in his coming don't cause us to lose faith. The loss of a sense of urgency, readiness, and faith in our response to Jesus's promise to return in power and glory is detrimental to our Christian walk.

Understanding that Jesus's return is imminent motivates us to live righteous obedient lives today. Remember in Luke 12:42–46 the unfaithful servant who said in his heart, "My master is taking a long time in coming," was surprised by the master's return and faced judgment. Let's make sure we are ready and living in a way that honors God today!

Each of us has to decide which path we will follow, and we need to decide today. Each day brings us closer to Jesus's return, and the decisions we make will have eternal consequences. God loves us and has made every effort to show us the right path. He has sent his Son so our sins could be cleansed and to make us righteous before Him. He has given his followers his Holy Spirit to teach and guide them so they might be sanctified. He has shown his love in immeasurable ways.

Yet God cannot and will not tolerate sin; sin is contrary to God's holy nature. Jesus said, "I am the way and the truth and the life. No one comes to the Father except through me" (John 14:6). That is what believing in God is all about. It is more than acknowledgment that there is a God; it is about submitting to his authority and making him Lord of our lives.

Today, let us choose to follow God.

ANSWERS TO BIBLE STUDY QUESTIONS

Chapter 1: A God of Covenants

1. will; actively
2. future
3. oath-bound
4. God's rule; creation
5. cursed; provision
6. humans and animals; flesh; murderers
7. nations; Israel; blessing
8. blessing; curse
9. dispersion; restoration; prosperity
10. forever; millennial; descendant
11. regeneration; forgiveness; knowledge
12. history; advance

Chapter 2: Seven Key Messages from Old Testament Prophets

1. a—forever; b—day of His wrath; judge; e—authority; power; everlasting
2. king
3. law; God; people; forgive
4. remnant; exiles; scattered people
5. spirit
6. destruction; wrath; salvation
7. knowledge; blossom

Chapter 3: Daniel's Vision of Future Kingdoms
1. a—gold; b—silver; c—bronze; d—iron; e— baked clay; f—rock
2. a—lion; b—bear; c—leopard; d—beast
3. a—ram; b—goat
4. Nebuchadnezzar
5. inferior
6. earth; four
7. crush; crushed
8. divided; little horn; kings; holy; times; law
9. Son of Man; crush; forever; dominion
10. a—restore; rebuild; b—Anointed One; c—abomination; desolation

Chapter 4: Other Prophetic Visions
1. military invasion; Holy Spirit; upheaval; final
2. judgment; restoration; Babylon; Egypt; millennial; new
3. restoration
4. judgment; heathen; remnant
5. remnant; Gog; temple
6. remnant; Jerusalem
7. Elijah's

Chapter 5: Jesus's Teachings on the Signs Preceding End Times
1. immediate; future
2. messiahs
3. wars, famines, earthquakes
4. saints
5. abomination that causes desolation
6. signs; wonders
7. upheaval

Chapter 6: Jesus's Return: An Event No One Will Overlook
1. lightning; sign; mourn; power, glory; elect
2. familiar; heavenly
3. near; unexpected; ready; faithful; wise

4. good; faithful; judgment; strangers; poor; sick

Chapter 7: Apostles' Teachings on End Times
1. know; clouds
2. church age; word; fire; patience; perish; holy; godly; grace; knowledge
3. Antichrist; Christ; like; test
4. saints; judge; scoffers; faith; pray; mercy

Chapter 8: Early Church Teachings on End Times
1. resurrect; caught up; sudden; armor
2. just; angels; everlasting destruction
3. alarmed; missed; man of lawlessness; Restrainer; perishing
4. godliness; truth; God-breathed; wise

Chapter 9: Preparing for the Lord's Return
1. watch out
2. alarmed
3. firm
4. flee
5. guard
6. witnesses; disciples

OLD TESTAMENT TEACHINGS ON END TIMES

New Covenant
- Chapters 1 and 2: Jeremiah 31:31–34—God will make a new covenant with the people of Israel; He will put his law in their minds and write it on their hearts; He will be their God, and they will be his people; He will forgive their wickedness.
- Chapter 2: Hebrews 8:6–13—Jesus is the mediator for the new covenant.
- Chapter 2: 1 Corinthians 11:23–32—Jesus's sacrifice on the cross made possible the fulfillment of the new covenant.

Outpouring of the Spirit
- Chapter 2 and 4: Joel 2:28–31—Outpouring of the Spirit on God's servants.
- Chapter 4: Ezekiel 37:4–14—Lord will put "breath" into the dry bones of Israel.

Abomination of Desolation
- Chapter 3: Daniel 8:9–14—Abomination that causes desolation foreshadows evil ruler in the end times.

- Chapter 3: Daniel 7:8–12, 20–25, 8:23–26—Led by boastful leader who emerges from ten kingdoms; wages war against God's holy people; take away daily sacrifice; leader who emerges is represented by little horn; see also Matthew 24:15; 2 Thessalonians 2:3.

Military Battles
- Chapter 4: Joel 2:1–11—Military invasion depicted as invasion of locusts; severe drought.
- Chapter 4: Joel 3:9–14—Battle in valley of Jehoshaphat; farm tools will be beat into weapons.
- Chapter 4: Ezekiel 38:1–5, 11–22—Defeat of Gog prince of Magog; battle against unsuspecting and peaceful people; God would defeat them with rain, hailstones, and burning sulfur.

Heavenly Upheaval
- Chapter 4: Joel 2:30–31—Wonders in the heavens and earth; blood and fire; sun turned to darkness; moon turned to blood.

Restoration of Israel
- Chapters 2 and 4: Isaiah 11:11–16—Lord will reclaim surviving remnant, gather exiles of Israel, and assemble scattered people of Judah.
- Chapter 2: Deuteronomy 4:25–31—If you become corrupt, the Lord will scatter you among the peoples; if you repent and seek the Lord, then the Lord will show mercy; the Lord will not forget his covenant with your ancestors.
- Chapter 4: Joel 3:1–3—Lord will restore the fortunes of Judah and Jerusalem
- Chapter 4: Micah 2:12, 4:1–5—Lord will bring together a remnant of Israel; establish the Lord's temple; nations will worship the Lord; weapons will be beat into farm tools.
- Chapter 4: Zephaniah 3:13, 20—Remnant gathered; will no longer sin or lie.

- Chapter 4: Ezekiel 34:13, 36:22–23—God will bring them out from the nations and gather them to their own land for the sake of his holy name.
- Chapter 4: Ezekiel 37:18–23—Israel and Judah will become one nation; Lord will gather them from the nations.
- Chapter 4: Zechariah 1:7–17, 1:18–21, 2:1–13, 3:1–10, 4:1–14, 5:1–4, 5:5–11, 6:1–8—Eight visions depicting Israel's deliverance from its enemies, restoration, and God's victory.
- Chapter 4: Zechariah 10:9; 13:7–9—Lord will save his people; they will return; one third remaining will be tested and refined.

Day of the Lord
- Chapter 2: Obadiah 1:15—Day of the Lord is near; your deeds will return upon your head.
- Chapters 2 and 4: Isaiah 2:17–18—Arrogance of humanity brought low; human pride humbled; only the Lord will be exalted in that day.
- Chapters 2 and 4: Isaiah 13:9–11—Day of judgment for the unrighteous and God's enemies.
- Chapters 2 and 4: Zephaniah 1:14–15, 3:8—Day of wrath; heathen nations will be destroyed.
- Chapter 2: Amos 5:18—Day of wrath.
- Chapter 2: Joel 2:32—Day of salvation.
- Chapter 4: Isaiah 13:19–22—Babylon and Egypt will be destroyed; Egypt will be healed.
- Chapter 4: Malachi 4:1–6—Evildoers will be punished; righteous will be healed; prophet Elijah will come to you before the day of the Lord comes; see Matthew 17:10–13.

Coming Redeemer
- Chapter 2: Genesis 3:15, 22:18—Redeemer will be seed of woman and Abraham; he will crush Satan.
- Chapter 2: Genesis 49:10; 2 Samuel 7:12–13—Redeemer will be from tribe of Judah and descendant of David; his throne will be established forever.

- Chapter 2: Deuteronomy 18:15; Zechariah 9:9; Psalm 110:4—Redeemer will be prophet, priest, and king; kings will be crushed on the day of his wrath; he will judge the nations.
- Chapter 2: Isaiah 7:14—Redeemer is Immanuel, God with us.
- Chapter 2: Isaiah 53:5—Redeemer will be a suffering servant.
- Chapter 2: Daniel 7:13–14—Redeemer will be a Son of Man; Messiah will come with the clouds; given authority and sovereign power; everlasting dominion.
- Chapter 3: Daniel 7:13–14—The Redeemer will come in the clouds with power and authority; everlasting kingdom.
- Chapter 4: Zechariah 14:4–9—Lord comes with his holy ones to Jerusalem; feet stand on Mount of Olives, splitting it in two; Lord will be king over the earth.

Kingdom of God
- Chapter 2: Psalm 47:2, 7—Lord is the great king over all earth.
- Chapter 2: Daniel 2:44–45—Kingdom will never be destroyed; it will crush other kingdoms and endure forever.
- Chapter 2: Psalm 2:2–6—King installed on Zion, God's holy mountain.
- Chapter 4: Ezekiel 37:24–28—David will be king over God's people forever; will follow God's laws; God's sanctuary will be among them.
- Chapter 4: Ezekiel 43:4–5—Sacrificial altar and temple restored; temple filled with the glory of the Lord.
- Chapter 4: Zechariah 8:3—Lord will return to Zion and dwell in Jerusalem.

New Heavens and Earth
- Chapters 2 and 4: Isaiah 11:6–9—Peace and harmony between humanity and animals.
- Chapters 2 and 4: Isaiah 35:1–10—Curse on ground lifted; desert shall blossom; springs of water.
- Chapters 2 and 4: Isaiah 65:17–25—New heavens and the new earth created; full of knowledge of the Lord.

Major Kingdoms Prophesied by Daniel

- **Babylonian Empire**—Chapter 3: Daniel 2:32, 37–38, 7:4; led by Nebuchadnezzar; represented in dreams by head of gold in statue and by lion with wings of an eagle.

- **Medo-Persian Empire**—Chapter 3: Daniel 2:32, 39, 7:5, 8:3–4, 20; Isaiah 13:17–18; Jeremiah 51:28; inferior to Babylon; represented in dreams by chest and arms of silver in statue, by bear with three ribs in its mouth, and by two-horned ram.

- **Greek Empire**—Chapter 3: Daniel 2:32, 39, 7:6, 17–18, 8:5–8, 21–22; defeats Medo-Persian Empire; given authority to rule; represented in dreams by belly and thighs of bronze, by leopard with four wings, and by shaggy goat with four horns; kingdom would be split between four rulers; Daniel 8:9–14—abomination that causes desolation foreshadows evil ruler in the end times.

- **Roman Empire**—Chapter 3: Daniel 2:33, 40, 7:7, 19–23; will crush and break the others; terrifying and very powerful; represented in dreams by legs of iron, by beast with large iron teeth and ten horns.

- **Ten-Nation Confederation**—Chapter 3: Daniel 2:33, 41–43, 7:7, 20–25, 8:17–26; led by boastful leader who emerges from ten kingdoms; divided kingdom; partly strong and partly brittle; wage war against God's holy people; take away daily sacrifice; represented in dreams by feet of iron mixed with baked clay and by ten horns on the beast; leader who emerges is represented by little horn; see also Revelation 13:5–7, 17:12–14.

- **Messianic Kingdom**—Chapter 3: Daniel 2:34–35, 44–45, 7:13–14, 26–27, 8:5–8, 21–22; will crush all other kingdoms; given authority, glory, and sovereign power; worshiped by all nations; everlasting kingdom; represented in dreams by rock cut out of mountain and Son of Man.

NEW TESTAMENT TEACHINGS ON END TIMES

False Messiahs

- Chapter 5: Jesus's teaching is in Matthew 24:4–5; Luke 21:8; Mark 13:5—There will be false messiahs. Don't be deceived. Don't follow them.
- Chapter 7: 2 Peter 1:3–19; 2 Peter 2:1–19—Traits of genuine versus false teachers are compared.
- Chapter 7: 1 John 2:15–27; 1 John 4:1–3—Antichrists will deny Jesus is Christ.
- Chapter 7: 1 John 4:1–3—Test the spirits to see if they are from God.
- Chapter 8: 2 Timothy 3:1–9—These men have depraved minds and oppose the truth.

Wars, Unrest among Nations, Famines, Pestilence, Earthquakes, and Heavenly Signs

- Chapter 5: Jesus's teaching is in Matthew 24:6–8; Luke 21:9–11; Mark 13:7—Wars, famines, and earthquakes must happen. They are the beginning of birth pains. Don't be alarmed.

- Chapter 5: Luke 21:11—Pestilence and great signs from heaven will occur.
- Chapter 5: Matthew 24:7; Luke 21:10; Mark 14:8—Nations will rise up against nations and kingdoms against kingdoms.

Persecution of Saints and the Spread of the Gospel
- Chapter 5: Jesus's teaching is in Matthew 24:9–14; Luke 21:12–19; Mark 13:9–13—The saints will be persecuted and die because of me. Some will leave their faith. The gospel will be preached to world. Stand firm in faith.
- Chapter 5: Luke 21:15; Mark 13:11—The Holy Spirit will give you words to speak.
- Chapter 5: Matthew 10:19–20—The Holy Spirit holds us up.
- Chapter 5: John 15:18–21, 16:2–4—They hate you because they hate me. A servant is not greater than his master.
- (Additional scripture) 1 Timothy 4:1–2—Some in the church will abandon their faith and be deceived.
- (Additional scripture) Matthew 10:16–33—Be on guard. Don't worry about what you will say. Some will be betrayed by family members. Stay firm in faith. Do not be afraid of those who can kill the body but not the soul. Whoever acknowledges me I will acknowledge.
- (Additional scripture) Matthew 16:27–28—Exhorts us to take up the cross and follow Him. When Son of Man comes in glory, he will reward each person according to his or her actions.
- (Additional scripture) Luke 12:2–53—Do not fear humanity; acknowledge God. The Holy Spirit will give you the words to say. Watch and be ready for Jesus's return. Families will be divided.
- Chapter 8: 2 Timothy 3:10–17—Those who want to live godly lives will be persecuted.
- Chapter 5: Matthew 24:14; Mark 13:10—The gospel will be preached to all nations and then the end will come.

- (Additional scripture) Mark 16:15; Matthew 28:19–20—The Great Commission: Jesus commanded his followers to preach the gospel.

Abomination That Causes Desolation in the Holy Place
- Chapter 5: Jesus's teaching is in Matthew 24:15–22; Luke 21:20–24; Mark 13:14–19—When the abomination of desolation appears in the holy place, those in Judea should flee to mountains. There will be great distress.
- Chapter 5: Luke 21:20—Jerusalem will be surrounded by armies.
- Chapter 7: 1 John 2:18—Another term used for this man is the Antichrist.
- Chapter 8: 2 Thessalonians 2:3–8—Jesus will not come until the man of lawlessness is revealed. This man will set himself up to be God. Jesus will overthrow and destroy him.

False Messiahs, Prophets, Signs, and Wonders
- Chapter 5: Jesus's teaching is in Matthew 24:23–26; Luke 21:20–23—There will be false messiahs accompanied by signs and wonders. Don't be deceived. Be on guard. If these days were not cut short, none would survive.
- Chapter 8: 2 Thessalonians 2:9—The man of lawlessness will use all sorts of displays of power through signs and wonders that serve the lie.

Heavenly Upheaval
- Chapter 5: Jesus's teaching is in Matthew 24:29; Luke 21:25–26; Mark 13:24–25—The sun and moon will be darkened. Stars will fall from sky. Heavenly bodies will be shaken.
- Chapter 5: Luke 21:25–26—The sea will be tossed. People will faint from terror.
- Chapter 5: Luke 23:29–30—People will say to the mountains, "Fall on us" and to the hills, "Cover us."

Jesus's Return in Glory and Power

- Chapter 5: Matthew 25:14–19; John 14:28–29; John 16:19–22—Jesus will go away and come back.
- Chapter 5: Matthew 26:64; Mark 13:26; Luke 21:27–28; Acts 1:11—Jesus will return in the clouds in power and glory.
- Chapter 6: Matthew 24:27–31—His return will be like lightning. There will be a sign in heaven. People will mourn. He will come in the clouds with power and glory. His angels will gather the elect.
- Chapter 6: Matthew 24:31; Mark 13:27—His angels will gather the elect.
- Chapter 6: Luke 17:26–27; Matthew 24:36–41: Like days of Noah—Jesus's return will be sudden. Some will be taken and others not.
- Chapter 6: Luke 17:28–33: Like days of Lot—People will be eating, drinking and marrying. His coming will be unexpected.
- Chapter 8: 1 Thessalonians 5:1–3—The day will come like a thief in the night. Destruction will come suddenly.
- Chapter 5: Matthew 24:32–35; Luke 21:29–33; Mark 13:28–31: Parable of Fig Tree— When you start to see the signs, you will know the time is near.
- Chapter 6: (verses below) Jesus's return will be unexpected and sudden.
  - o Matthew 24:42–44; Parable of thief—Destructions will come suddenly; keep watch and be ready.
  - o Matthew 24:45–51; Mark 14:32–36: Parable of servants—Be ready. Be faithful and wise.
  - o Matthew 25:1–13: Parable of ten virgins—Be ready.
- (Additional scripture) John 5:24–29— Jesus promises eternal life to followers. He references the resurrection of the dead at his return.
- (Additional scripture) John 6:39–40—Jesus promises eternal life. The dead will be resurrected. None who has been given to Jesus will be lost.

- Chapter 7: Acts 1:3–10—No one knows the timing of Jesus's return. Be my witnesses. Make disciples of men.
- Chapter 7: Acts 3:11–26—Jesus will be in heaven until the time comes for his return.
- Chapter 7: 2 Peter 3:1–6, 8–9—The delay in Jesus's return reflects the patience of Lord not wanting any to perish.
- Chapter 7: 1 John 3:1–3—When Christ appears, we shall be like him.
- Chapter 7: 1 Corinthians 15:51—We will be raised imperishable at the last trumpet.
- Chapter 7: Jude 14—The Lord is coming with thousands of his holy ones. He will judge everyone.
- Chapter 8: 1 Thessalonians 4:13–18—First the dead will be raised, and then the living, to join Christ when he returns.
- Chapter 8: 1 Thessalonians 5:1–4—The day of the Lord will come like a thief in the night.
- (Additional scripture) Hebrews 9:23–28—When Jesus returns, he will do away with sin and bring salvation.

End of Age
- Chapter 5: Matthew 25:14–30: parable of bags of gold—Be good and faithful servants. There will be judgment at the end of the age based on your actions.
- Chapter 5: Matthew 25:31–46: comparison of sheep and goats—Live obedient lives. Show compassion for strangers, poor and sick.
- (Additional scripture) Matthew 13:40–43, 49–50—judgment will be at the end of the age. Weeds will be thrown in the fire. Good fish will be separated from the bad.
- Chapter 7: 2 Peter 3:7–13—The earth will be destroyed by fire. There will be a new heaven and earth.
- Chapter 8: 2 Thessalonians 1:8–10—God will judge those who do not know God and do not obey the gospel of the Lord.

- Chapter 8: 2 Thessalonians 1:7— Jesus will be revealed in heaven in blazing fire with his powerful angels.
- (Additional scripture) 1 Corinthians 15:24–28—He will hand over the kingdom to the Father. Satan's army of angels and death will be conquered.

How Should We Respond to These Events?

- Chapter 9: Matthew 24:4–5—Watch out that no one deceives you.
- Chapter 9: Matthew 24:6—Don't be alarmed.
- Chapter 9: Matthew 24:13–14—Stand firm in faith. Preach the gospel of the kingdom as a testimony to all nations.
- Chapter 9: Matthew 24:15–16—For those in Judea, flee to mountains.
- Chapter 5: Matthew 24:23–26—Don't believe lies of the false prophets and messiahs.
- Chapter 9: Matthew 24:42–44—Keep watch. Be ready.
- Chapter 6: Matthew 25:14–30—Be good and faithful servants.
- Chapter 6: Matthew 25:31–46—Show compassion for strangers, the poor, and the sick.
- Chapter 9: Luke 21:34—Be careful. Be always on watch. Pray that you will escape all that is about to happen and that you may be able to stand before the Son of God.
- Chapter 9: Matthew 28:19—Make disciples of others. Teach them to obey what I've taught you.
- Chapter 9: Acts 1:8—Be my witnesses. Make disciples of men.
- Chapter 7: 2 Peter 3:11–18—Live holy and godly lives, growing in grace and knowledge of our Lord. Be on your guard so you won't be deceived.
- Chapter 6: Jude 20–23—Build yourselves up in faith and pray in the Holy Spirit. Keep yourselves in God's love. Be merciful to those who doubt.
- Chapter 7: 1 Thessalonians 5:5–10—You are children of light. Be sober. Put on faith and love as a breastplate and the hope of

salvation as a helmet. Encourage one another and build each other up.

- Chapter 7: 2 Timothy 3:15—Study the scriptures, which are God-breathed and able to make you wise for salvation.
- (Additional scripture) Philippians 4:5–7—The Lord is near. Stand firm in faith. Don't be anxious, but pray. God's peace will guard your hearts.
- (Additional scripture) Titus 2:11–14—Live godly while you wait for the blessed hope.

ABOUT THE AUTHOR

DeLinda N. Baker was raised a Christian. She attended the University of Texas at Austin and majored in accounting; she graduated in 1977 with a bachelor's degree in business.

Toward the end of her sophomore year in college, DeLinda felt the tug of the Holy Spirit and made a commitment to follow and live for Jesus. From that day on, her life began to change as God began to work in her life.

Professionally, DeLinda started out in accounting and then became a technical consultant assisting companies in moving manual accounting processes onto computerized systems. For the remainder and bulk of her career, she was a project manager for technical, process, and merger initiatives for a major national bank. In this capacity, she moved up in rank until she retired in 2015.

Spiritually however, DeLinda began to discover different gifts and desires. Early in her walk with the Lord, among those gifts, she found she had a deep desire to teach. While initially she led Bible studies developed by other authors, she later began to develop her own studies on topics that plagued Christians and were often misrepresented in our culture. This book represents one of those studies related to the signs of Jesus's return. Her passion in teaching is to be true to the Word of God and to not add or subtract from the teachings of scripture.

DeLinda has served as deacon for numerous years in her church, actively participated in the leadership of the women's ministry, led Sunday school classes, and assisted with administrative and financial projects in the church.

ENDNOTES

1 David Jeremiah, *Agents of the Apocalypse: A Riveting Look at the Key Players of the End Times* (Carol Stream, IL, Tyndale, 2014), 197–198.

2 *Wikipedia,* "2015 kidnapping and beheading of Copts in Libya," https://en.wikipedia.org/wiki/2015_kidnapping_and_beheading_of_Copts_in_Libya.

3 *Christianity Today*, "After Removing 400 Crosses, China Proposes Where Churches Can Put Them Instead," http://www.christianitytoday.com/gleanings/2015/may/after-removing-400-crosses-china-proposes-zhejiang-wenzhou.html.

4 Billy Graham, *Storm Warning* (Nashville, TN, Thomas Nelson, 2010), 16.

5 George Bush, address before a joint session of the Congress on the state of the union, January 28, 1992.

6 Beth Moore, *Daniel: Lives of Integrity: Words of Prophecy* (Nashville, TN, LifeWay Press, 2006), 40 in workbook.

7 https://www.merriam-webster.com/dictionary/covenant.

8 Charles C. Ryrie, *Dispensationalism* (Chicago, IL, Moody Press, 1995), 41.

9 Peter J. Gentry and Stephen J. Wellum, *God's Kingdom through God's Covenants* (Wheaton, IL, Crossway, 2015), 251.

10 Anthony A. Hoekema, *The Bible and the Future* (Grand Rapids, MI, William B. Eerdmans Publishing Company, 1979), 3.

11 "What is the day of the Lord?" https://www.gotquestions.org/day-of-the-Lord.html.

12 Will Durant, *Our Oriental Heritage*, 224.

13 *Wikipedia,* "Nebuchadnezzar II," https://en.wikipedia.org/wiki/Nebuchadnezzar_II.

14 Bible History Online, "The Babylonian Empire," http://www.bible-history.com/maps/03-babylonian-empire.html.

15 Charles C. Ryrie (Chicago, IL, Moody Press, 1986), *The Ryrie Study Bible: New International Version,* 1175.

16 *The Bible Knowledge Commentary of the Old Testament*, 1359.

17 *Wikipedia,* "Achaemenid Empire" https://en.wikipedia.org/wiki/Achaemenid_Empire.

18 *Ryrie Study Bible*, 1180.

19 Ibid.

20 Bible History Online, "Map of the Persian Empire," http://www.bible-history. com/maps/maps/map_persian_empire.html.

21 *Wikipedia*, "Roman Empire," https://en.wikipedia.org/wiki/Roman_Empire.

22 Bible History Online, "Map of the Roman Empire," http://www.bible-history. com/maps/maps/map_roman-empire.html.

23 "What is the significance of the Medo-Persian Empire in biblical history?" http://www.gotquestions.org/Medo-Persian-empire.html.

24 *Ryrie Study Bible*, 916.

25 Clay Watts, *Preparing for End Times: Major Old Testament References to End Times—Isaiah*, http://www.claywatts.com/endoldt.htm.

26 *Ryrie Study Bible*, 1242.

27 Ibid., 1263.

28 Tim LaHaye and Thomas Ice, *Charting the End Times: A Visual Guide to Understanding Bible Prophecy* (Eugene, OR, Harvest House Publishers, 2001), 91.

29 *Wikipedia*, "Gog and Magog," https://en.wikipedia.org/wiki/Gog_and_Magog.

30 *Ryrie Study Bible*, 1643.

31 *Daniel: Lives of Integrity—Words of Prophecy*, by Beth Moore, 150–151 in workbook.

32 Ibid.

33 Ibid.

34 Ibid.

35 *Ryrie Study Bible*, 1657.

Printed in the United States
By Bookmasters